MISSION COLLEGE
LEARNING RESOURCE SERVICE

THE
SILENT SPEECH
OF
POLITICIANS

BODY LANGUAGE IN GOVERNMENT

by
M.D. Blum, Ph.D.

Illustrated by Patrick Neill

BRENNER INFORMATION GROUP
San Diego, California

The author and publisher have researched all available sources to ensure the acccuracy of the information contained in this book. However, we assume no responsibility for errors, inaccuracies, omissions, or any other inconsistency. Any slights against public figures or organizations are unintentional. The descriptions of the body language used by people in the text, photographs, and illustrations contained in this book are based on the professional expertise of the author and are not the responsibility of the publisher.

FIRST EDITION
FIRST PRINTING - 1988

Published by :   Brenner Information Group
                 13223 Black Mountain Rd.
                 Suite 430
                 San Diego, California 92129

ISBN: 0-929535-00-6

DEDICATION

To Jay, who struck while the iron was hot

DATE DUE

NOV 7 '91		
NOV 21 '91		
MAY 27 1994		
NOV 27 2002		

ACKNOWLEDGEMENTS

I appreciate the opportunity to publicly recognize the contributions of the following people: Robert C. Brenner, whose positive attitude and optimism made working on this book a pleasure at all times; Lee Rathbone for her extremely sensitive and highly effective text editing; Renée Mancini at *Time Magazine* for her guidance with photo syndication; Jacques at Woodfin Camp for his cooperative spirit; and the artist Pat Neill, for his sense of humor.

On the personal level, I express gratitude to the friends and family members who have been so well-meaning during the anti-sociality of this authorship: Sharon Blum for her daily love; Ira and Sylvia Perry for their constant concern; my husband Jay, the best partner I could ever have; Stephanie Weber for always listening and for her practical responses to emotional trauma—mine; my neighbors, the Petersens, the Herring-Spencers and the Nakais, who invited me to dinner when I was too strung out to feed myself; and Marty, who gave everything possible.

CONTENTS

Books are written for many purposes. This book was written to be meaningful on several levels. First, *The Silent Speech of Politicians* conveys information dealing with communication, politics, and pyschology. These topics have deep importance for all of us who want to direct our own lives.

Few would argue that an enhanced ability to communicate can improve the quality of life. How much more satisfying and less frustrating our lives would be if we could express ourselves clearly while understanding the expressions of others clearly, too. This book is intended to help you communicate better.

Politicians have great influence on our daily lives. Many of us have longed for some form of yardstick that would help us make increasingly intelligent choices about the people we select to represent our interests. It's my belief that this book can and will help you make better choices by enabling you to more accurately "read" a politician's true character. If, through this book I can help you feel better equipped to make election decisions, then I will have achieved my first purpose — to make a meaningful contribution to society.

Views on the merits of psychology are as varied as people themselves. Psychology, psychotherapy, and even competent, ethical psychotherapists (yes, they do exist) are still considered by many as elements in the lives of "others" who experience severe emotional distress or "mental illness." In reality, modern psychology is a highly demanding, scientifically rigorous profession designed to promote personal growth and improve the quality of life for individuals, families, communities, and societies, both distressed and healthy.

Improving interpersonal and cross-cultural communication is a legitimate and central concern of modern psychology. The information in this book is intended to contribute to a better appreciation of what psychology is and how it can be used in a "healthy" context.

The second purpose for my writing this book is to present meaningful material in as concise and readily usable form as possible. In my opinion, most books — even very good books— are too long. I intended this book to be no longer than necessary. It is designed so its message can be digested in an evening or on a business flight, and its content put to use immediately. The information in this book is practical and concrete. If you walk away from your reading with something specific that you can apply, then my second purpose is fulfilled.

What makes a book "good?" It must be useful, entertaining, or thought-provoking. If the information that follows stimulates your thinking about nonverbal communication and the psychology of politics, and if you enjoy reading *The Silent Speech of Politicians,* then a third purpose is fulfilled, and I have written a "good" book.

M.D.B.
Colorado Springs, Colorado
June 26, 1988

CHAPTER 1

The Silent Speech of Politicians

*The idea that you can merchandise candidates for
high office like breakfast cereal...is the ultimate
indignity to the democratic process.*
— *Adlai Stevenson*

Introduction

Our world has become an amazingly tiny ball of intricately interconnected communication networks. Telephone lines span the most remote corners of civilization. Television instantly and simultaneously brings the drama of war or famine into a million comfortable living rooms far across the globe. Teletype gives immediate feedback on who buys or sells whom. The sophistication and rapid growth of communication technology is mind-boggling.

Somewhere behind the wizardry and magic of communication technology are the communicators, the people for whose sake all this gadgetry exists. Because the earth has become so communicative, because information—all kinds of information—is transmitted virtually at the speed of light, communicators at all levels of societies and cultures everywhere have had to become more sophisticated themselves. Because there is so much information to convey, speakers have had to become more effective at streamlining their ideas to the most powerful form possible, in the shortest time possible. Because the eyes and ears of the world have become as large and as acute as the most sensitive telescopes and amplifiers imaginable, the presentation of that information must be precise, specific, and unambiguous.

In the early 1940s, families huddled around a squeaking, scratching fuzzbox, straining to catch the tinny words of the latest war news. Today, multiple televisions in various rooms of a middle-class home compete for the attention of anyone present, offering "spectrasound," "omnivision," or 25 inches of high density resolution. As communication media have become increasingly realistic and unforgiving of the messages they convey, attention has come to be focused on refining the "soft" technology of the message itself. The "how" of the message has become as important as its "what," and the would-be effective communicator must be skillful at manipulating that "how" for public consumption.

Public figures around the world, political and popular, are the royalty of the blossoming communication science. It is their message, their ideology, their dogma which is converted into electrons and disseminated by wire, wave, tube, and screen to the far reaches and vast masses. Consumers of the media are the beneficiaries of this royalty, looking, listening, observing, reflecting, measuring, and evaluating the messages they receive, judging politicians and entertainers by the quality of their presentations.

Politicians and entertainers have a lot in common in this new wave of communication technology, and they have much to learn from each other. Entertainers have always known that audiences are sensitive to certain nuances of behavior that accompany what is being said. These nuances are largely comprised of gestures and postures that are powerful *nonverbal* communicators. Politicians have learned, through experience, that the various electronic media distort these nonverbal communicators in specific ways that can enhance or severely limit the effectiveness of a presentation. It is speculated that one reason Richard M. Nixon lost the 1960 U.S. presidential election to John F. Kennedy was that Nixon wore the wrong color shirt in the televised, pre-election debates. Nixon's white shirt gave him a yellow appearance compared to Kennedy's light blue, which against the dark blue backdrop of the debates gave Kennedy a radiant aura that communicated power—before a word had even been uttered. Look closely and you will notice that these days, most American politicians wear light blue collars for TV appearances. ✳

If politics has taught media moguls something about image management, the entertainment industry has taught bookloads about nonverbal communication to politicians. This book is about the nonverbal communication behavior of political figures. But lest the reader be misled, be aware that virtually *all* politicians are coached by someone, usually from the entertainment industry, about the proper gestures, postures, and mannerisms to use in public. However, the trained eye can discern a distinct silent message in the gestures and mannerisms of even the most experienced public actor—for this is much of what politics is all about.

Understanding Body Language

Most of us believe that since speaking and listening are things we have done since birth, we are, prima facie, experts at it. In reality, all of us communicate, but *good* communication is a skill acquired through instruction, thoughtfulness, and diligent practice with feedback. Smooth nonverbal communication takes even greater attention to detail, since the significance of wordless messages is more subtle, more subject to interpretation.

At the turn of the century, Charles Darwin, the tireless cataloger of animal lore, chronicled his observations of consistent patterns of facial expressions across species and across societies. Darwin asked questions about the expression of such diverse emotions as astonishment, rage, and pleasure, and found *universally identical gestures displaying these feeling states.*

In the 1940s and 1950s, serious scholars began investigating the components of nonverbal communication, the gestures, postures, movements, and personal mannerisms that say so much without a word being spoken. The early work of anthropologist Edward T. Hall led to the development of the study of "proxemics"—the communication value of the use of personal space. Perhaps even better known than Hall is Professor Ray L. Birdwhistell, who coined the term "kinesics" to denote the field of study interested in identifying the meaning of individual gestures. Hundreds of books and articles have been written on the scholarly significance of nonverbal communication.

In 1970 Julius Fast published his popular book, *"Body Language."* Suddenly there was a revolution in consciousness. The study of nonverbal communication was out of the ivory tower, available for everyone to explore and use, and everyone wanted to know more. Fast made an important contribution to the public utility of silent language by making the clear point that postures, gestures, and other signals had to be interpreted in the light of their *context.*

The significance of Fast's observation that body language, like all communication, must be interpreted against the background of what's being said, who's talking, and whatever else is going on around, must not be undervalued. We take it for granted that context clues will fill us in to the proper meaning of verbalizations. Yet, observers and self-proclaimed experts of body language are eager to assign a single specific meaning to particular gestures. This just cannot be done. A person who stands in the midst of a group, displaying the highly visible gesture of arms crossed tightly in front of the body may be signalling defensiveness or closed mindedness. It's also possible that the person is cold. Or has a weak back. Or feels impatient about the proceedings and wants to go home. Or maybe it's just a comfortable way for this person to stand at this time and place.

How then does one make sense of gestures? What are the meaningful context variables that contribute to an accurate interpretation of silent speech?

Gerard Nierenberg and Henry Calero, authors of *"How to Read a Person Like a Book"* (Simon & Schuster, 1971), are businessmen who have conducted exhaustive field studies about nonverbal communication, particularly in business settings such as sales negotiations. Nierenberg and Calero found that in addition to context, accuracy in interpreting the silent language of gestures and postures is dependent upon recognizing *clusters* of behaviors surrounding verbal communications. Single gestures taken in isolation more often than not communicate an incomplete or inaccurate story. *Groups* of gestures interpreted as a whole provide the context to support correct translation of gestures into meaningful language.

A final concept that is of critical import in understanding body language or nonverbal communication is *congruence*. Congruence represents the consistency of what is being said and how it is being said. Silent language tends to have a greater truth value than does verbal language. When in doubt about how to interpret a verbal message if its nonverbal accompaniments seem to be saying something else, go with the nonverbals. Allan Pease, author of *"Signals: How to Use Body Language for Power, Success and Love"* (Bantam, 1984), asserts that "bodies don't lie," even when words do.

Establishing congruence is a key to understanding nonverbal communication, and behaving congruently is essential to effective silent language. If you've ever gotten the feeling that someone was sending you "mixed signals," it's possible you were on the receiving end of incongruence between words and gestures. Your ears told you one thing, but your eyes told you something very different. Incongruence signals untruth. Incongruence makes listeners uncomfortable.

How To Use This Book

Dr. Albert Scheflen, another noted author on body language, suggests that out of the myriad of gestures, postures, and mannerisms humans emit, only a limited number have significance as communicators—possibly fewer than thirty gestures in all. In this book I have tried to identify those gestures and gesture clusters that are prominently displayed by political figures as they go about their business in the public eye. I have isolated six broad groups of gestures exhibited by politicians that span the gamut from emotional states to executive qualities. Within each of these six categories I have detailed specific gestures and their meanings, with illustrations from historical and contemporary political figures, presenting a total of about seventy gestures, including variations in the display of common movements.

At the end of each chapter is a summary of all the gestures detailed in the chapter itself, a quick way to keep the meaning of various movements fresh in your mind as you observe your favorite (or least favorite) politician in action. At the end of the book is a checklist of desirable and undesirable silent communicators frequently observed among political figures. With the checklist, you can quickly assess for yourself how skillful, congruent, and genuine the person you are observing is as a communicator. Use the book to educate yourself about the language of gestures. Then put your newfound knowledge to the test by analyzing the gestures of political figures you observe in the media.

Still life media such as photographs from magazines or books are easiest to use as you begin your study of silent speech, because the gestures get "frozen." The speakers hold still, in a sense, long enough for you to think about the significance of their body language and to reach a conclusion about its meaning. Live appearances and video performances are much more challenging, but once you become familiar with the most frequently displayed signals, even the character of a very active politician will reveal itself to you, especially if you make good use of the checklist in Chapter 8. I think the insights you will gain from this practice will be of benefit in terms of the decisions you make, the conclusions you draw, and the attitudes you maintain about the world in which you live.

CHAPTER 2

Defensiveness

*If you don't say anything, you won't be called
on to repeat it.*
— *Calvin Coolidge*

The Meaning of Defensiveness

On a scale of desirable personality characteristics defensiveness scores low. In fact, defensiveness is considered undesirable in most interpersonal situations. "Defensive" is a word we hear a lot, to describe someone not present, to put down someone who is present, or to put a defensive-prone person on the defensive in order to gain power over them. But what does it really mean?

Defensive behaviors and postures reflect an inner state of insecurity. Defensive people are unsure of themselves. That's why they're defensive—they are trying to protect themselves from scrutiny, criticism, or perceived threat from others. A defensive person is either lacking in a base of self-confidence or *wants to hide something* from others.

Sometimes people are defensive when they have said something they can't or don't want to explain. Translate the psychological term "defensive" into the phrase "defend self" and you have a good understanding of what a defensive person is trying to accomplish. Defensiveness hardly seems appropriate for a political representative.

Another reason defensiveness is not a desirable characteristic in a politician is its association with closed mindedness. A protective,

Fig. 2-1. A classic defensive stance is seen in the crossed arms and crossed legs of this politician.

secretive power broker who also may have a tunnel vision value system seems more likely to breed bigotry and discontent than harmony between peoples. Such a person is unapproachable and inflexible. Are these the best qualifications for a national or international negotiator and dispute settler? More likely, defensiveness might contribute to the nature of a tyrant, dictator, or hard-line extremist.

Politicians who are coached in the subtleties of body language are instructed to resist their bodily temptation to display defensive gestures, but only a very crafty, very careful, and *very* defensive politician could completely keep from ever showing the tell-tale signals of defensiveness. The body doesn't know how to lie.

Crossed Arms

The obvious signal for defensiveness is the commonplace posture of arms folded across the chest (Figure 2-1). Charles Darwin expressed the belief that this gesture had universal identity of appearance and meaning in every country in the world. However, it is very rare that you will find a prominent U.S. politician in this stance. One highly notable exception is *Time Magazine's* April 11, 1988 cover of U.S. Democratic presidential nomination hopeful Jesse Jackson. It remains a mystery to me why Jackson allowed himself to be captured in this pose, which historically, to be sure, may have been identified with men of power, but which today expresses virtually the opposite.

Up to and including the time of Dwight Eisenhower, powerful statesmen were often posed and painted or photographed in this posture. It may have been considered a symbol of resolve, granite determination, a nonverbal "nobody fools with me" communicator. But since the publication of Professor Ray L. Birdwhistell's research on nonverbal communication in 1952, the true meaning of the arms folded in front of the body has been widely disseminated.

Domestic body language coaches evidently tell their political students that such mannerisms are interpreted by the observant public as meaning, "I'm hiding something." In this day of honesty in American politics, a defensive posture puts off confidence and votes.

Foreigners, however, are another case. Middle Eastern, Asian, Latino, and European politicos have been glimpsed publicly in this gesture. Muammar Kaddafi, the caustic Libyan leader, can frequently be found posing with his arms crossed in front of his chest. Reuter Press captured a sample of this telltale nonverbal signal when Kaddafi allegedly threatened to kill Ronald Reagan in 1987. Furthermore, Mr. Kaddafi will also often make a fist with one or both hands when his arms are thus crossed, signifying an angry, frustrated, or belligerent attitude (Figure 2-2).

Another version of this defensive, arms-crossed-in-front-of-body stance includes grabbing the upper arm with the hands of the crossed arms. This gesture makes a clear statement about a need for security on the part of the individual using it.

Ironically, while politically savvy members of our society refrain from making this crossed-arm defensive display in public, represen-

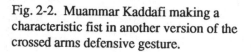

Fig. 2-2. Muammar Kaddafi making a characteristic fist in another version of the crossed arms defensive gesture.

tatives of the finance industry and of the medical industry are often photographed in such a pose. Like politicians, these people are sometimes in the position of saying things that may be conjectural. Who knows how the bond market will fare? How sure can a medical examiner be that a self-inflicted death is intentional or accidental? When pressed to explain themselves or give proof for their statements, they may cross their arms in front of their chest in a silent attempt to protect themselves from criticism (Figure 2-3).

When evaluating a politician for signs of defensiveness, be sure to look for the "thumbs-up" detail (Figure 2-4). Although there is still an element of closedness in this posture, the person who uses it is also sending confidence and optimism signals, saying on the one hand,"I feel threatened," but on the other, "I can handle it." A speaker who is covering up the truth may add this detail unconsciously, saying in effect, "I know I'm going to get away with this."

By contrast, shy people, unaccustomed to publicity, who are experts in their fields, may use the detail superimposed on the arms-

Fig. 2-3. "Clutching" suggests a need for security.   Note how the hands are exposed over the crossed arms in this version of the defense gesture.

Fig. 2-4. The exposed thumb signals confidence.

crossed nonverbal expression of discomfort as a way of stating, "I may be quiet but I can sure get the job done." Financiers, too, include the thumbs-up detail. In their case it may mean, "There are no guarantees (but *I've* made a lot of money this way)." Women rarely point their thumbs up when crossing their arms unless they are crossing simply to keep warm.

A final caution: a person who is tired, who has been standing a long time, or who has a bad back, may assume this position to relieve backstrain and provide some structural support. In this case, "arms crossed" may mean, "Let's get this over with," or—it may not mean anything at all!   •

Defensive Legs

Arms crossed in front of the body is the most obvious nonverbal signal of defensiveness, but many more exist. Legs may be crossed above the knee or below the knee. Ankles may be locked. Heels may be held closely together in a rigid military position.

The seated position lends itself well to nonverbal defensiveness cues. A person who sits back in the chair is creating maneuvering distance in a conversation or dialogue. A seated person can shift to face away from someone with whom they become uncomfortable, without appearing rude. What could possibly be more defensive than turning a chair back to a person in a conversation and straddling the chair seat? The chair back becomes an effective barrier or shield between the conversants.

Gerald Nieremberg and Henry Calero in *"How to Read a Person Like a Book"* point out the intimidating effect the chair back has on a conversation. Allan Pease, author of the nonverbal communication guide, *Signals*, suggests that if you expect a visit by someone who habitually confronts you with a chair back, having a chair with arms as the only other one in the vicinity will prevent this maneuver. Here is a psychological insight to add to your body language library of information: a person who consistently acts in a threatening, intimidating way, especially while manifesting defensiveness signals, is really a "scaredy cat," with more hiss than scratch. Call their bluff—if *you* have the confidence.

I am reminded of a story that was told to me when another psychologist and I were putting together a women's assertiveness training workshop several years ago. The co- therapist, Joan, invited a female deputy sheriff from the town where the workshop was being conducted to participate, thinking she might be a good role model. The policewoman responded to Joan's invitation by ceremoniously straddling a chair, whipping her jacket away from her hip as she did so (Figure 2-5). The butt of her revolver showed plainly. Said the Deputy Sheriff, "I don't need to be assertive; I carry a gun." She did not attend the workshop.

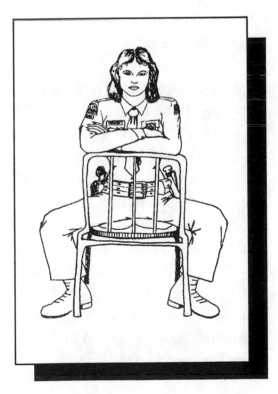

Fig. 2-5. People in this pose can be assertive or defensive.

Fig. 2-6. In the Figure Four, the leg makes a shield for the body.

The Figure Four

Ray L. Birdwhistell, a hallmark researcher in nonverbal communication, made students of kinesics, the study of gestural components, aware of a posture he named "the Figure Four." A uniquely American pose, the Figure Four (Figure 2-6) is a comfortable way of sitting, with one leg propped up on the knee of the other. It also effectively creates a barrier between the one using the Four and other people. The Four is acceptable for women in slacks, as well as for men, though it is not used as much by women.

Sitting in the Figure Four signifies argumentativeness and competitiveness. It may also alert an aware observer to the possibility of defensiveness—as would any barrier posture. Holding the leg or the knee with hands clasped in the Figure Four accentuates its defensive value (Figure 2-7).

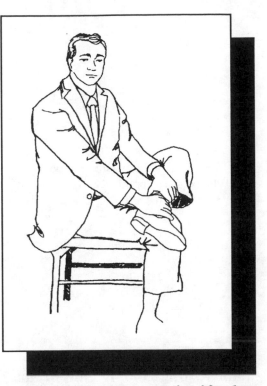

Fig. 2-7. The Figure Four with Holding is comfortable because the user feels protected.

Remember, a defensive type pose may not always signify that emotional state. When interpreting body language, it is imperative to read the context at all times. For example, a person who uses the Four to sit while clasping hands behind the head, elbows up and out, with a small smile on his face is actually expressing superiority, not the need for a barrier. The Figure Four can just as readily express confidence and *absence* of defensiveness as another, less desirable state (Figure 2-8). In American politics, you are more likely to see the Four being used among outgoing and secure individuals than as a posture of weakness.

Barriers that Communicate

Like a chair back or the upper leg in the Figure Four, many barriers are available as accessories to defensiveness. A politician who shakes

Fig. 2-8. In this Figure Four pose, the person's upper body signals confidence.

hands while holding "important" papers in front of the body with the left hand is in effect saying, "I come in peace...but I don't trust you entirely."

When Richard Nixon met Leonid Brezhnev in Moscow in 1972 to sign peaceful co-existence agreements between the two superpowers, the men signed their respective copies of the treaties and then shook hands. Brezhnev held his hard cover copy of the agreement under his arm like a schoolboy carrying a book; Nixon placed his hardcover copy between his body and Brezhnev's, reaching *over* the booklet to shake hands (Figure 2-9). The treaty booklet became an effective, defensive shield for Nixon. His maneuver may have contradicted his warm smile and hand clasp, saying nonverbally, "I welcome this meeting, but I still feel a need to protect myself from you."

Nixon's defensiveness in this context may have been appropriate. How much can the Americans trust the Russians? If the Soviets know that American presidents come in peace but are not gullible, they may

Fig. 2-9. Nixon used a book as a barrier providing him with a feeling of protection from his political adversary.

be more motivated to negotiate sincerely. A wise opponent is worthy of respect.

Any interpersonal action can be thought of as occurring in a space. The area between the people engaged in the action, whether the players are facing each other or not, is the "inside" of the interaction. The area surrounding the interaction, such as people's backs when they are facing each other, is the outside. Other barriers that may be placed "inside" a communication are a shoulder, a handbag, a wine or cocktail glass, or a coffee mug, especially if the item is held with two hands.

A final class of defensive gestures is one with a double meaning. People who peer over the tops of their eyeglasses may be using the spectacles as a kind of psychological barrier. Glasses wearers sometimes feel "masked" while wearing their glasses and unmasked or naked without them. The glasses acquire a reassuring quality, making their owner feel defenseless without them. Peering over the

Fig. 2-10. Peering over eyeglasses like Senator Hatfield may put others on the defensive.

glasses is also a critical, judgmental gesture. Many people are uncomfortable being looked at this way, "down someone's nose," as it were. What better way to defend self than to be offensive to someone else?

Joan Rivers is famous for this over-the-glasses stare. In 1984, Senator Mark Hatfield of Oregon, a distinguished politician with an unimpeachable reputation for honesty, found himself under investigation by the FBI and the Senate Ethics Committee concerning monies earned by his wife Antoinette and a possible connection with the Alaska pipeline. Hatfield, too, has a habit of peering over his eyeglasses while testifying or presenting to the Senate on a variety of issues (Figure 2-10). Does the behavior of Rivers and Hatfield signify defensiveness? Consider the contexts in each case and decide for yourself.

Summary: Defensiveness

Defensiveness means unsureness about oneself or about a situation. Defensive people are trying to "defend self" from perceived harm, attack, criticism, rejection, or investigation. People lacking in self-confidence display defensive behaviors. Defensiveness is generally a highly undesirable trait for a politician.

Gestures	Meaning
Arms crossed in front of chest	Protecting self, shielding, closing oneself off
with hands in fists	Belligerence, aggressiveness, frustration
grasping opposite arms	Needing security, reassurance
with one or both thumbs up	Defensiveness with superiority
Legs tightly crossed, standing or sitting; ankles locked, heels locked	Protecting self, "keeping one's own ground," keeping to oneself, not telling
Straddling chair backwards	Shielding oneself, domineering personality, false confidence

Gesture	Meaning
Seated Figure Four	Creating a barrier
Interposing a shoulder, papers, handbag, wine glass	Creating a barrier
Looking over tops of eyeglasses	Criticalness as offensive defensiveness; judging

Notes on Nonverbal Communication: Defensive Threats

A person who acts in a threatening way designed to intimidate, but who simultaneously displays defensiveness, is likely to be bluffing, using this behavior as a protective device against threatening behavior by other people. The threats of a huffing, puffing politician who hurls insults with arms crossed tightly across the chest are generally not to be believed.

CHAPTER 3

Confidence

Do what you can, with what you can, where you are.
(or: walk softly and carry a big stick)
                                        —Theodore Roosevelt.

Certainly a prime requisite for leadership is confidence—in one-self—and the ability to instill confidence in the constituency. While a defensive politician might want to hide signs of insecurity, the confident individual expresses positive energy and openness with both words and body gestures. The great orators of the world's political history have typically been confident personalitics. Confidence is an important nonverbal communicator to look for when attempting to "read" a politician. Fortunately, it's an easy one to spot.

Hands on Hips

Conjure up an image in your mind of a stoic George Washington making his frigid foray across the Delaware River to fight for independence and found a great nation. Can't you just see him at the prow of his tiny vessel, the wind in his face, his cape swept back from the hand at his hip while his proud, hawklike nose points the way to destiny?

The hand-on-hip gesture is one of a small group of powerful nonverbal communicators that speak clearly about self-confidence (Figure 3-1). Recognized by the body language experts as a consistent signal in the human species, its roots have been hypothesized to come

Fig. 3-1. The classic sign of confidence.

from self-enhancing behaviors among other animal species. Darwin noted that birds fluff themselves up to look more powerful to predators or adversaries and to look more attractive to same genus birds of the opposite sex. More attractive birds have a better chance of mating, so their genes get passed on. There we have it—survival of the fluffiest.

When a human bird—rooster or hen—puts his or her hands on hips, an illusion of greater size is created. The gesture can translate into, "I am powerful," as a confident person might believe. Marketing pros in the clothing industry are well aware of this, which is why you see so many models with hand at hip. Supposedly, it makes the clothing look better because the wearer looks more powerful. Everyone loves a winner.

The hand-on-hip gesture also signals two other nonverbal messages: "I am ready," as was the gunslinger of the wild west with his half-curled hand poised near the butt of his pistol; and "I am unafraid." The hand-on-hip gesture bares the vulnerable frontal portion

Fig. 3-2. When Mondale stood with his jacket open and his hands on his hips, he signalled confidence.

of the human body. Such a gesture, willingly and comfortably executed, suggests courage. The impact of the stance is accentuated when the well-dressed politician unbuttons the jacket of his two piece suit and then puts hand to hip. The suit jacket flares wonderfully (as does George Washington's cape in the mentally constructed scene above) to enhance the wearer's image of stature and power. Walter Mondale, who figured prominently in the media in 1984, was often seen in this confident pose (Figure 3-2). Had silent speech been the ticket, Mondale's body language should have been enough to carry him to the White House. He was ever the picture of perfect body language.

Woodrow Wilson, lecturing at the turn of the century at Columbia University, referred to himself and other U.S. presidents as "...a small class of...wise...athletes..." He punctuated his remarks with a haughty hand-on-hip pose. Winston Churchill was observed in 1922 striding ferociously up a beach at Deauxville in full length bathing wear—*both* hands on his hips!

Fig. 3-3. Donald Trump's hand at his belt calls attention to a confident, centered attitude.

The confident, hands-on-hip stance seems to wordlessly, but loudly, proclaim one's readiness for direct action. A related gesture, a slightly more discreet one, is composed of a thumb or two hooked into the belt. Donald Trump is an interesting figure in the public eye. He may or may not go political. He almost never poses for a photograph without a hand at his hip or touching his belt (Figure 3-3).

The Articulate Thumb

Having once heard it, one could never forget Alan Alda's eloquent *"Mash"* episode on the human articulated thumb. Yes, thumbs are interesting gadgets, and myths abound about their significance, but one story that is no myth is that thumbs signal confidence.

An upturned thumb has diverse meanings in many cultures around the world. In the political arena, it neatly symbolizes optimism and superiority, both of which are associated with confidence. The thumb is flicked upwards to display delight in an outcome on the campaign trail, exuberantly expressing success. More subtly, it rests along the

Fig. 3-4. Winston Churchill's hand at his lapel says, "I believe in myself."

lapel of a winner like Winston Churchill, emphasizing his belief in his right to lead (Figure 3-4)

When the thumbs are tucked into one's armpits or suspenders, their presence is only implied, not clearly displayed. But doesn't this picture (Figure 3-5) create the perfect image of proud confidence and

Fig. 3-5. Churchill demonstrating proud confidence and happiness.

Fig. 3-6. George Bush showing a hesitant "thumbs-up." While thumbs up gestures generally signal confidence, the message here suggests a plea for reassurance. (Photo by Dennis Brack/Black Star)

happiness in your mind's eye?

Thumbs up signals with the palms facing inward toward the face of the signaller reflect reserved happiness, such as in the case of George Bush after the New Hampshire presidential primary (Figure 3-6). Thumbs up with outspread arms, palms facing out, shout incredulously, jubilantly, "I won!"

Nineteen eighty-eight seemed to be "The Year of the Thumb." Well-coached American politicos, from U.S. President Ronald Reagan to Teamster's Union President Jackie Presser all utilize the powerful nonverbal signal. Similarly, Evan Mecham, the ex-governor of Arizona, used the gesture to emphasize confidence in his eventual acquittal from prosecution.

The 1988 U.S. presidential nomination campaign was particularly full of thumbs. Here is a body language expert's analysis of this campaign's "thumbs in politics":

Fig. 3-7. Michael Dukakis uses his thumbs to reassure the public that he is confident. (Photo by Steve Liss/Time Magazine)

The thumbs of George Bush were rather less convincing than his beaming incredulity of Super Tuesday. His thumbs-up signal was tentative, questioning, almost shy. Rather than stating emphatically, "I am assured," his thumbs seemed to ask, "Will you reassure me?"

The thumbs of Governor Michael Dukakis are classically, academically correct. These are Harvard inspired thumbs. Only...they don't project inspiration. These are confident, sure thumbs, but the emotion they convey is carefully regulated, formal, not insincere, just a little stiff, the thumbs of a man in control of his emotions (Figure 3-7).

Mr. Dukakis appeared to pick up his thumbs to express a particular image, not the excitement of the campaign trail. There's nothing really wrong with that—President Reagan is the consummate master of image politics and it never seemed to hurt him a bit (Figure 3-8).

The Reverend Jesse Jackson is another case. Mr. Jackson is an astute observer of human behavior. His campaign momentum was

Fig. 3-8. President Reagan uses his thumb
to signal victory.

based not so much on responsible representation of the issues, but on intelligent image management and high-voltage oratory resulting in tremendous emotional appeal. He thereby distinguished himself from all the other presidential hopefuls and gave voting Americans something personal to which they could relate as individuals. Jesse made us feel important, not because of what he said, but because of how he made us *feel*.

It is a mistake to attach secondary significance to the value of nonverbal and "subvocal" communication signals in the political arena. The content of a politician's message is barely heard above the din emanating from the *manner* of presentation. Would Winston Churchill have won the hearts of the world if he looked like Woody Allen? Would Martin Luther King's "dream" have captured the imagination of white and black Americans alike had he pronounced his vision in a squeaking soprano? Doubtful.

Jesse Jackson has great thumbs. Palm readers might say they show creativity and passion. Indeed, Jackson was cited again and again in

Fig. 3-9. Jesse Jackson's thumbs-up signal says, "I feel good. Why not join me?"
(Photo by Marc PoKempner)

the media for expressing passion that the other contenders appeared to lack. Jackson must *know* he has a great thumb because he used it as Winston Churchill or Richard Nixon used the V for Victory sign—as a personal signature, a vehicle to express himself and reach The People. Bush said, "I'm one of you," and showed his thumbs. Jackson said, "I *am* you," and got everyone around him to show *their* thumbs (Figure 3-9).

Here's another tidbit from the records of the psychologist for your personal library of nonverbal communication: when a person has a feeling to express, the body will reveal the feeling state by any number of subtle and gross physical signals. When displaying certain specific body signals, a person *will* experience the associated feeling state.

To understand this better, try the following exercise: Stand with shoulders slumped, head down and belly out. Observe how you feel. Your psyche will feel heavy, depressed in this stance. Now stand proudly erect with shoulders back and chin high. Notice your feeling state. Chances are you *will* feel good. This is basic body/mind synergy. It's a good topic to elaborate on—in another book.

If a fundamental task of the successful politician is to express confidence and *instill confidence*, what better way to make this happen than to model the appropriate body behaviors and get those you are trying to influence to emit them, too? By now the media embargo on anti-Jackson remarks is lifted and everyone knows that Jackson's apparent campaign success was not based on political astuteness, managerial effectiveness, or rational problem-solving, but on raw emotional appeal. Jackson was the one nomination hopeful who was able to get large masses of people to identify with him emotionally *and feel good about doing it.*

Thumbing

Thumbs can convey another message, though. When someone "jerks" a thumb toward another, it is a message of ridicule (Figure 3-10). Allan Pease, author of *Signals*, found this to be a simple way to simultaneously acknowledge someone's existence and put them down, without getting your own foot stuck in your mouth. Mention the person by name or category and jerk your thumb in their direction, present or implied, and you lower their status in the minds of your listeners. The jerked thumb serves the same purpose in the adult world as "thumbing the nose" does for children, a slightly more sophisti-cated way of saying, "Nyah, nyah, nyah."

In November 1987, Mikhail Gorbachev of the Soviet Union visited Czechoslovakian President Gustav Husak to discuss Gorbachev's reform program, *peristroika*. Gorbachev jerked his thumb at Husak while everybody had a good laugh. Shortly after, Husak announced his plans to resign, for health reasons. Could the powerful Russian's nonverbal put-down have signalled trouble for the ailing Czech?

Fig. 3-10. "Thumbing," or "jerking the thumb:" an adult putdown.

V for Victory

Body language is really very easy to understand, once you learn some basic rules. I have observed in my practice that, in general, gestures involving movements up and away from the center of the body have positive connotations or are used by confident, dominant individuals. Negative messages are sent by those gestures involving downward, inward movements. Thumbs up are positive; slumped shoulders are not. Shoulders out and back show confidence and self-esteem, while arms crossed tightly in front of the body express just the opposite.

One of the clues then, that thumbs up may relate to confidence is the upward, outward movement of the gesture. In 1941, Winston Churchill introduced what was to become his world-famous signature: two upraised fingers signifying victory. Churchill's V for Victory is an

Fig. 3-11. Churchill's famous "V for Victory" gesture also signals self-confidence.

upward and outward movement (Figure 3-11). The gesturing hand is held out from the body, usually at shoulder height or above, and the fingers point up in the direction of optimism. Other, less laudable hands-out-fingers-up gestures not withstanding, Churchill's victory sign also sent a message of confidence and optimism.

Other politicians since Churchill have been able to capitalize on the power that the remarkable British statesman invested in this hand signal. Think of Richard M. Nixon on election eve 1968, or driving in his motorcade amid a blizzard of tickertape. Surrounded by adoring thousands, Nixon thrusts his arms skyward, his fingers stabbing triumphantly upward in the clearly recognized symbol of victory (Figure 3-12). Amid the din of a cheering crowd, the fingers up for victory also signals acceptance of tribute to a powerful and confident leader. Asserting confidently that he was going to bring America back together again, Nixon gladly, exuberantly accepted the love of the voting public (though his actual victory margin was slim).

Fig. 3-12. Nixon adopted Churchill's confidence gesture and made it his own trademark.

Steepling

"Steepling" is another term credited to Ray L. Birdwhistell, one of the pioneer researchers of nonverbal communication. Steepling is the word Birdwhistell used to describe the gesture of leaning the tips of the outstretched fingers of both hands against each other, creating an image reminiscent of a church steeple. The body language researchers are largely in agreement that steepling is a clear confidence communicator.

When a person in a private session with me displays this behavior and I ask what they are feeling, I can get a range of responses. If however, I phrase my question in a leading way such as, "I sense you're feeling pretty confident about what you've just said...," I will invariably get an affirmation. If the person does not verbally confirm confident feelings, the steepling generally stops when I ask the question this way.

Fig. 3-13. The high steeple demonstrates strong expressive confidence.

Four forms of steepling have been observed in the body language literature: standard steepling, the high steeple, the low steeple, and a variety of subtle steeples. The standard steeple cuts across a variety of situations. Pease found that high steepling, with the hands held in front of the upper third of the body, tends to occur in very confident people or in confident people while they are talking (Figure 3-13). By contrast, low steepling, with the hands at waist high or lower, or with fingers pointing down, takes place when a normally confident individual is in a receptive or listening mode.

Mikhail Gorbachev, the Soviet general secretary, can be observed steepling in any number of circumstances (Figure 3-14). He steeples in Moscow. He steeples in Washington. He steeples when he listens (Figure 3-15). He steeples when he talks. He steeples high. He steeples low. He even steeples when he smiles. And he uses the subtle steeple, too. The world sees Gorbachev and marvels at his poise, whether he is folk dancing in Czechoslovakia, negotiating at a

Fig. 3-14. The steepled fingers of Mikhail Gorbachev signal quiet self-confidence.

summit, or scrambling down an embankment to a potato farm in Mother Russia. Gorbachev himself sends the silent but clear message, "I'm in control here; I'm comfortable."

Subtle steepling occurs when the fingers of the steepled hands are folded slightly over each other, or the hands gently cup each other, but the inverted "v" form of the steeple remains. Jesse Jackson held his hands in a modified or "subtle" steeple while he waited for American and Cuban hostages to be released in 1984. Evidently he believed his mission would be a success. John Ehrlichman steepled subtly when he talked about impeachment proceedings. He knew what he was saying.

Lt. Col. Oliver North steepled subtlly during Iran-*contra* hearings in 1987. Was he confident that the system he supported would now support him, or did he have an ace to play? Was he signalling his confidence in his eventual absolution, or was he simply confident that, no matter what, he wasn't going to suffer too badly—at least not

Fig. 3-15. While listening, Gorbachev's lower steeple suggests a receptive, but confident frame of mind.

alone? Ollie North certainly seemed to possess some inner conviction that sustained him through the sometimes stormy, often tedious hearings. He expressed that confidence to a watching, spellbound nation, with his subtly steepled hands (Figure 3-16).

People in money industries don't seem to bother with the subtleties of modified steepling—they simply stretch their fingers, tip them together, and state their case. Politicians, who may be more sensitive to public response than financiers, understand the value of nuance. Furthermore, a successful politician is one who matures rather than just ages. Winston Churchill replaced the flamboyant, almost haughty hands on hips and hand on lapel gestures of his early career with truly elegant, simply understated, modified steepling in his later years (Figure 3-17). The steeple—a powerful nonverbal indicator of confidence among today's politicians.

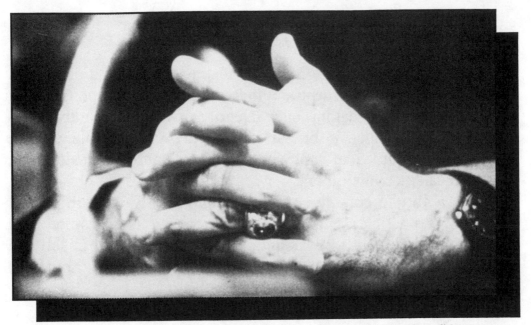

Fig. 3-16. Lt. Col. Oliver North's folded steeple speaks silently of self-confidence. (Photo by W. McNamee/Newsweek)

Fig. 3-17. Churchill in an elegant modified steeple radiates his self confidence.

Summary: Confidence

Confidence is a highly desirable characteristic for a politician. Confidence is a central issue in any individual's self-concept. Courage, conviction, decision-making, even integrity all relate to an individual's self-image. A confident politician is one who is comfortable with the responsibilities of leadership, who can accept control of a situation, and who can motivate others.

The ability to convey confidence nonverbally is an important aspect of a politician's expressive repertoire. The gestures and movements that silently speak about a politician's belief in self and mission are clear, definitive, and easy to read—once you know how.

Gesture	Meaning
Hands on hips or hands at belt or thumbs in belt	Confidence, readiness for action; sexual readiness
Thumbs up	Confidence, optimism, superiority, happiness in success, triumph;
Hands on lapel	Confidence, belief in ability to lead, superiority, arrogance
Hands in armpits or under suspenders	Implies the presence of thumbs as above, subtle
Thumbing, jerking a thumb, or thumb to nose	Ridicule
Two-fingered V sign	Positive connotations—optimism, confidence, accepting confidence from others, accepting position of authority
Steepling	Confidence, superiority
—high	—talking mode, possibly dogmatic belief in self
— low	— listening mode, open

Gesture	Meaning
— subtle (variations)	— quiet confidence, mature

Notes on Nonverbal Communication: Body/Mind Synergy

There is a cooperation of the body and the mind known as synergy. Synergy means all the parts work together, enhancing each other. One of the ways the synergy of body and mind is expressed is through nonverbal communication. What a person feels, the body will express nonverbally. However, the synergy, the co-operation between the body and the mind, works in both directions, so that when a person assumes a certain posture, or gesture, the mind feels the related emotion and reacts. When you smile you feel happier than when you frown; when you frown, you feel less happy than when you smile. Try it.

CHAPTER 4

Clasping

The only thing we have to fear is fear itself
— Franklin Delano Roosevelt

There is a class of hand signals related to confidence signals that is diverse enough to merit separate consideration. This class is comprised of the variety of movements involving clasping of the hands.

Clasping, in its standard form, looks very much like a subtle steeple, but it actually denotes the opposite of the steeple's confidence. A person who tightly intertwines the fingers and clasps the hands together, wrings the hands, or "holds one's own hand" is nonverbally expressing worry, concern, doubt, or need for reassurance—very much the opposite of the steeple.

To properly read a politician or other public figure, one must be very attentive to the subtleties differentiating clasping and steepling. Both categories are frequently displayed in public settings, and both are prominent and noticeable. The difference between a steeple and a clasp can sometimes be difficult to discern.

The first clue to look for in telling a clasp from a steeple is evidence of hand pressure. Taut skin on the fingers gives the impression of "white knuckles." Steepling does not cause this phenomenon. In modified or subtle steepling, the fingers are loosely intertwined, not locked or squashed against each other. Everyone knows that white knuckles speak of a stage prior to outright panic. Just think of so-called white knuckle drivers or white knuckle fliers you may know. Idioms such as these creep into our daily vocabulary as our awareness of how the body and the mind work together increases.

Fig. 4-1. The tightly clasped hands of Frank Carlucci suggest inner tension or worry. (Photo by Dean Rutz/ The Washington Times)

I was temporarily misled by a photograph of Frank Carlucci, the secretary of defense who replaced Caspar Weinberger under the Reagan administration. The photo captured Carlucci with a calm face, his hands folded neatly in front of him in what appeared to be a modified high steeple (Figure 4-1). "What a confident, mature, self-assured individual this Carlucci is," I thought. However, when I re-examined the photograph, I noticed that the skin of Carlucci's fingers was bunched up around his knuckles from the pressure of his clasped hands. I then realized Carlucci has a poker face. He has undertaken a difficult job—and he knows it, too—but isn't outwardly admitting concern. He is able to keep his face impassive, but his hands give him away.

A person who holds one finger in front of the body with the tips of the other hand, or who "fidgets" with a fingertip, fingernail or cuticle, is displaying doubt signals. Gorbachev steeples. He has a broad repertoire of steepling gestures. Reagan gently touches or holds the prone fingers of his right hand with the tips of his left hand. Which superpower leader conveys greater confidence in himself?

Answer: Gorbachev. He steeples artlessly wherever he is seen. Reagan is much more studied in his nonverbal behavior. His mannerisms have the fluid look of conscientiously practiced lessons. Thus the Russian seems to be a "natural athlete of the hand signal," while the American president commits only to what he has learned is useful. Gorbachev's steepling is a consistent, prominent part of his nonverbal vocabulary. Since Reagan is seldom seen in steepling or steeple-like gestures, his hand-to-hand signals are not likely to be modifications of the classic form of this move.

Modifications of the intense, white-knuckle clasp abound. One may clasp one's own wrist in front of one's body with the opposite hand. Richard Nixon did this when he was in the company of other prominent politicians such as Henry Kissinger or Mao Tse Tung (Figure 4-2). Around the Watergate boys he displayed different signals. Tammy Faye Bakker was photographed in a seated version

Fig. 4-2. Nixon's "Hand-In-Front-of-Body" clasp could have been an anxiety signal.

Fig. 4-3. Kurt Waldheim in his own version of the "Hand-In-Front-of-Body" clasp.

of this exact pose when interviewed after the "Praise the Lord" scandal broke.

Austrian president Kurt Waldheim is rarely photographed today without some semblance of a clasping gesture (Figure 4-3). Waldheim goes so far as to actually clasp one fisted hand with the other, which may be signalling frustration and aggression as well as doubt and worry (Figure 4-4).

Michael Jackson, a current figure of public interest and one who is often seen with prominent political figures, is a character around whom much debate has been generated. His critics are quick to point out that the young star's idiosyncrasies are tantamount to elite snobbery, that his reclusive habits make his adoring fans only burn all the more to see him. But look at Jackson's body language (Figure 4-5). While performing, the artist who has been exposed to the glare of footlights since single-digit age appears to be the model exhibitionist,

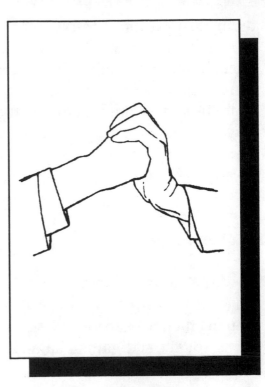

Fig. 4-4. Holding a fist with the other hand suggests frustration or aggression.

Fig. 4-5. Michael Jackson's clasped hands say silently that, despite his ability to perform on stage, he is really an introvert.

daring to make moves on stage only now beginning to be emulated by other hopeful up- and- comers. Yet off stage, Jackson is hardly ever interviewed or photographed without accompanying clasp gestures, some subtle, some not. It's highly likely that Jackson, beaming supreme self-assurance amid leathers, buckles, zippers, and glitter on stage is really a retiring, shy introvert, who craves most of all reassurance from his audience that he is acceptable, lovable, and loved.

Hidden Fingers

Another variation on the clasp consists of clenched hands with fingertips turned inward. In this pose, the tips of the fingers are actually hidden from view. Late in 1987, Costa Rican president Oscar Arias sought and gained an audience with Ronald Reagan. Arias

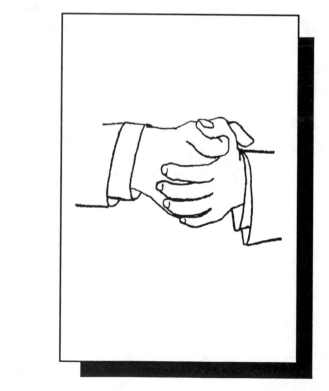

Fig. 4-6. Hidden fingers suggest a hidden agenda.

wanted the United States to stop supporting the *contras*, and came citing instances of increased democratization among the Sandanistas. But the handsome Arias sat with his legs locked in an aggressive Figure Four pose, with his hands clenched tightly in a finger-hiding clasp (Figure 4-6). Arias was awarded a Nobel prize for his landmark peace-making efforts, but I would have to wonder about a diplomat whose body language was so competitive, closed, and worried.

Women in Politics

Women in general tend to be more emotionally expressive than males. In many cases, the nonverbal behavior of women is more interesting to observe than that of men. Geraldine Ferraro was a wonderful exemplar of nonverbal expressivity in 1984. Before she was selected, but after she knew she was being considered as a vice

Fig. 4-7. Holding her own hand, Geraldine Ferraro seems to be seeking reassurance.

Fig. 4-8. When clasping shifted to steepling, you knew Ferraro had become confident.

presidential running mate for Walter Mondale, she conferred with other politicos such as Tip O'Neill and displayed classic hand-holding gestures (Figure 4-7).

Once it became highly likely that Ferraro was going to be Mondale's choice, she appeared before reporters, shielding her body from the public with an armful of papers, as if to say, "I still need to protect myself from these guys." After Ms. Ferraro had been informed of Mondale's choice, she appeared before a microphone with classic, high steepling hands, confident of her qualifications for veepdom (Figure 4-8). That was 1984. What a year.

Also in 1984, then Prime Minister of India, Indira Gandhi was photographed in the hand-holding clasp. A subtle detail, though, appeared in her hands—the thumb of her left hand was slightly separated from the rest of her hand, with a decidedly upward cast to its separation. The complete message, then, might read something like, "I am confident I can lead my country, only sometimes I'm not so sure of my methods." Hundreds of citizens died under the harsh measures Mrs. Gandhi imposed to maintain control. Riots flared sporadically but numerously throughout the land and the resident regime was harshly criticized, both domestically and abroad. Yet, Indira Gandhi managed to maintain a form of working democracy in the poor, beleaguered, multi-lingual country. Given this setting, Mrs. Gandhi's mixed message was not so far-fetched.

Formal Authority

Clasping shows its relation to steepling in yet another way. A distinct category of confidence signals involve a specific kind of clasping. These are the authority confidence signals. When an individual bares the front of the body by holding the hands behind the back or head, an inner feeling of confidence is displayed that comes from a belief in the individual's right to authority. Hands slipped into back pockets, or thumbs hooked over the edge of back pockets may have the same "brave" meaning.

Hands clasped behind the back is a gesture often observed in persons in the military or in law enforcement. These individuals are invested with clearly codified and sanctioned authority. George Shultz, U.S. secretary of state under the Reagan administration and a former Marine, uses this stance. Shultz is able to negotiate and facilitate worldwide because he knows he has the authority to make important decisions (Figure 4-9).

Schultz is nonverbally expressive in another classic way. He is seldom seen without his hands in some sort of clasp pose. Initially, Shultz's hand-to-hand grip impresses one as clenched hands signifying self-doubt. But given the enormity of the task Shultz has undertaken in mideast peace facilitation and his unrelenting tenacity at the job, even as a likely lame duck emissary, a closer look at his hands is warranted.

Fig. 4-9. The "Hands-Behind-the-Back" pose of George Schultz is typical of people who believe in their own authority.

Schultz is an interesting case. The amount of hand pressure in Schultz's clasp is impossible to determine from media coverage. That's how inscrutable the man is. In 1983, a year after Schultz had taken over from Alexander Haig, cronies in the White House were crooning that Schultz lacked the initiative, power, or confidence to make things happen in the State Department. Given that his frequently displayed clasped hands could have meant that Schultz doubted himself and needed reassurance, administration officials could have been correct in their assessment.

Schultz has just as often been observed in an unambiguous classic steeple as he has in what seems to be a clear hand clasp. Because of this, we are safe in assuming that Schultz does feel self-confident. This lends a confident context value to the meaning of his clasping. Thus while clasping usually signals anxiety, when used by a person we already know is strong, centered, and confident, an apparent clasp may just be a relaxed form of a modified steeple. Schultz has allowed powerful men to be added to his staff without abdicating his authority. Detractors have criticized Schultz for being passive, but where more aggressive politicians have left their posts, Schultz remains. Passive? Perhaps, but serene, self-assured and confident, just as likely.

Arrogance

Only a confident and secure individual is comfortable with hands behind the back, but self-confidence and personal security can be taken to extremes. When the hands of a confident gesturer move upward from behind the back to the head level, watch out for an attitude of confidence waxing to smug superiority.

Examples of this pose in politicians are less noticeable than among other public figures. Money moguls, for example, often display this smug superiority posture, with feet on desk, to boot. Arnold Schwarzenneger, unparalleled seven-time Mr. Olympia, the pinnacle of men's bodybuilding, appears perfectly comfortable leaning back in a chair, elbows out, hands clasped neatly behind his well groomed head, his powerful biceps and prominent tooth gap clearly displayed (Figure 4-10). Arnold has not only immortalized himself in the annals of bodybuilding, claiming a domination of the sport unmatched in history, he has also established himself in the world of cinema, in elite social circles, and as a businessman in his own right. One could conclude that any self-made millionaire, even one with less laurel than Schwarzennegger, has cause for smugness.

Clasp and Steeple

A final class of clasp gestures needs elaboration. This is the sometimes confusing hand signal that combines clasped third, fourth, and fifth fingers with steepled index fingers.

Fig. 4-10. The "Hands-Behind- Head" pose of Arnold Schwarzennegger signifies a very high degree of self-confidence, possibly to the point of arrogance.

This is also a superiority gesture. I have seen it displayed by clients in private sessions when they believe they have an ace to play in a conflict situation. Arrogant, elite, or highly accomplished individuals will make this gesture, with the added detail of holding the steepled index fingers to their lips, when they are waiting for another person to finish talking. This signals their attempt to "hold their tongue" until it becomes time for them to express their own superior opinion (Figure 4-11). I have also seen the steepled index fingers levelled at another person, almost like a gun. In context, the clasp and steeple is an aggressive superiority gesture.

The clasp and steeple will be discussed further in Chapter 7, when we explore gestures that involve touching the face and gestures that accompany the decision-making process. Many gestures convey multiple meanings and, as with spoken language, silent speech must be interpreted in context. In one context, a clasp and steeple with index fingers held to the lips may be a signal of superiority. In another

Figure 4-11. The clasp and steeple is an aggressive superiority gesture.

setting, at another time, or used by another person, the gesture may indicate confidence about a decision to "say no more."

Summary: Clasping

Clasped hands and hands holding hands are prominent nonverbal signals that may appear to mimic other gestures. Clasping runs the gamut of meaning from self-doubt to aggressive superiority. Because of the similarity in appearance of clasp gestures and other nonverbal communicators, clasping must always be interpreted within the context in which it appears. Then it may have great value in helping the interested observer understand the character and motives of the person with the clasped hands.

Gesture	Meaning
Tightly clasped hands Fidgeting with fingertip Grasping a finger Picking at cuticle Holding one's own hand Grasping one's own wrist	Self-doubt, need for re-assurance, worry
Grasping one's own fist with other hand	Holding back frustration and aggression
Hidden fingers	Keeping something back
Hands behind head	Superiority, smugness
Clasp and steeple	Arrogance, aggressive

CHAPTER 5

Get My Point?

Voters quickly forget what a man says
—Richard M. Nixon.

Another very important cluster of nonverbal signals to consider when evaluating a politician are the aggression/frustration communicators. A key vehicle for insight to a person's character is the way they handle emotion, especially strong emotion such as anger.

Aggressive politicians are vehement about their beliefs; they draw a hard line and stand behind it. Interested more in "winning" than in world opinion, an aggressive politician may be a strong leader, but also a dogmatic totalitarian.

Aggressive individuals tend to be easily frustrated. People who emphatically want to have their way are typically impatient, especially when circumstances work to thwart their designs. Like the heart-attack prone "Type A Personality," such persons are easily angered, and in fact, often *are perpetually* angry. Though there may be something attractive, even compelling, about the zeal with which an aggressive statesperson pursues an objective, a politician with these traits may lack the diplomatic flexibility and finesse to be truly effective in the complex arena of national or world affairs.

The character of a frustration-fraught individual is molded by renegade emotions. Such a person lacks a serene center and tends to be reactionary, stimulated by outside factors rather than internal motivation. A genuinely confident person is outgoing, strong-willed, possibly heavy-handed , but is not antagonized by disagreement, unexpected difficulties, or even failure. A confident person, a true leader, is flexible, welcoming adversity as a way of forging true conviction out of consensus. An easily frustratable, aggressive, domineering, rigid, and belligerent public figure is threatened by anything less than abject acquiescence because, at root, this person lacks a fully integrated, internally-centered base of self-esteem.

A frustration prone and aggressive person is likely to vent this frustration on others—either personally or in the political context. This is not a healthy substrate upon which to base decision making, negotiation, planning and development. Thus, signals of frustration and aggression are noteworthy when evaluating the body language of prominent persons.

Two distinct types of signals relate to an aggressive or frustrated personality. These are the fist and the pointing finger.

The fist was recognized by early peoples as a symbol of aggression. The American Indian used an upraised fist to symbolize fearlessness and power, especially in combat contexts. The upraised fist became a familiar contemporary symbol of power and passionate self-respect as Black consciousness and pride grew in America.

If 1988 is the Year of the Thumb, 1968 may be remembered as the Year of the Fist—an elated year, an angry year, a year of anguish, turbulence, tension, chaos, a year of victory, a year of shattering defeat and disillusionment—a year silently but powerfully commentated by a fisted salute from America's elite, her Olympic medalists (Figure 5-1).

In the body language lexicon, showing the fist, or implying the presence of a fist, may mean a range of things, but it always speaks about strong emotion. Determination, anger, vehemence, resolve, and defiance all have been determined to be signalled by fist signs. Like clasping, fisting may reveal frustration or defensiveness. When the context supports it, fisting, like clasping, may signal confidence and strength. The spectrum of fist meanings can be broken into three categories, each of which is represented by its own particular type of fist gesture.

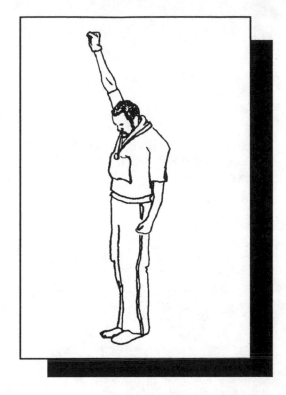

Fig. 5-1. In 1968, American Olympic medalists gave the salute of power gesture.

Shaking the fist

In this gesture, the fist is used almost like a hammer. Adolph Hitler was infamous, for among other things, his use of a shaking or pounding fist to emphasize the strength of his angry aggression. With his shaking fist, the dark, crazed, reactionary wizard of genocide "stamped" his rhetoric with the heavy hand of his perverse dogma (Figure 5-2).

Nikita Krushchev and Soviet diplomats pounded the tables at the United Nations to aggressively manifest disagreement. Kruschev, a volatile reformist, was another great fist shaker.

The Upraised Fist

As in the salute or the battle sign, the upraised fist represents triumph and power or affirmation, much like upraised thumbs. But

Fig. 5-2. Adolf Hitler's agitated fist added emphasis to his agitated words.

Fig. 5-3. Manuel Noreiga's upraised fist suggests an angry tyrant.

Fig. 5-4. The way Kadaffi holds his fist by the other hand is a negative sign. It means anger is present and is barely held back.

the fist makes a much more intense statement than thumbs. Hence, where the upward and outward movement of "thumbs up" or the "Victory V" has the positive and desirable connotations of optimism and confidence in winning, the jubilantly upraised fist of Gen. Manuel Antonio Noriega, the Panamanian dictator, may reflect aggression running to vicious despotism (Figure 5-3).

Clasped Fist

A fisted hand clasped by a person's other hand, is generally considered to be a highly negative sign. The gesture communicates an attempt to hold back frustration or anger. Often the person who uses this gesture is unaware of the anger, although it is clearly expressed to informed observers.

An outstanding political example of this gesture is Muammar Kaddafi, the avowedly reformed terrorist from Libya. The warlike

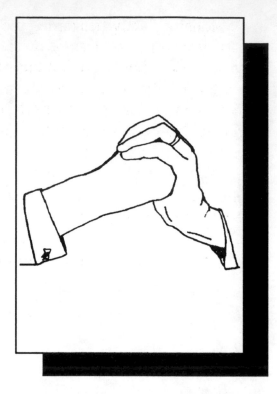

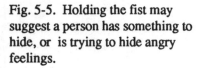

Fig. 5-5. Holding the fist may suggest a person has something to hide, or is trying to hide angry feelings.

Libyan talks about reconciliation among his politically estranged neighbors and muses innocently about Ronald Reagan (whom he publicly attempted to disgrace) *while clasping his fisted right hand*! Kaddafi failed to ingratiate himself with other North African leaders by repeated acts of disaffection. Now he purports to have mellowed and is seeking to strike neighborly bargains. Would you buy a used goat from this man?

Another striking example from public life, also one with possibly troubling implications, comes from Kurt Waldheim, the troubled president of Austria and former secretary-general of the United Nations. The clasped fist suggests holding back of angry feelings, perhaps with something to hide. Waldheim has been observed in numerous clasping gestures, including a fisted clasp virtually identical to Kaddafi's (Figure 5-5).

Waldheim was accused of participating in acts constituting war crimes during World War II. The questions of impropriety surrounding Waldheim's activities during the war have caused an unfavorable light of world opinion to shine on the small country of Austria. Waldheim has been denied invitations to the usual round of diplomatic affairs that typify the calendar of a president of a sovereign nation, and he has been seldom visited by other heads of state. Exceptions? Waldheim has been welcomed by the Pope and a handful of Muslim countries—including Libya.

Holding the wrist of a fisted hand is another variation of the fisted clasp. The meaning of this gesture is similar to the covered or clasped fist. This gesture was observed in one G. Gordon Liddy, American tough guy. Similarly, hands balled up into fists thrust deeply into pockets tell of thinly veiled anger or aggression.

Fist-to-Chin

In this gesture, the fist implies strength. Aggression is not always bad, as it implies goal directedness and the vigor to reach even difficult goals. However, *angry* aggression may be a danger signal in a political figure. A fisted clasp or a supporting fist may indicate a capacity for restraint or grim resolve. A well-known strong man with a "commando" persona, Arnold Schwarzennegger poses with his fist to his jaw to express his tough mindedness in business. James Baldwin, the firey Black author, was also observed in this pose, an apt personification for a gesture of barely restrained rage. But the fist-to-chin gesture, as most other nonverbal cues, needs to be read in context; one would hardly perceive Rodin's "Thinker," the famous statue with a fist-to-chin pose, as an image of anger.

Get to the Point

Modified fist gestures are the nonverbal communicators involving a pointing finger. While the fist is not often seen in formal settings, probably because its overpowering symbolism may be considered impolite in politics, pointing is everywhere in evidence.

Pointing largely replaces fisting gestures, without much difference of meaning. Pointing imparts emphasis to a verbal communication. Allan Pease, author of *"Signals: How to Use Body Language for Power, Success and Love,"* believes "the pointed finger is a symbolic club with which the speaker figuratively beats his listener into submission." Pointing is an annoying nonverbal communicator. Like showing the fist, pointing reflects frustration, generally frustration with the person at whom the point is directed.

In politics—and in sermonizing—the impact of the point is diffused throughout the audience, crowd, or congregation, but its meaning is not diminished, even if it does become more rhetorical. And politicians can be seen pointing everywhere.

Richard Nixon was a famous pointer. Even before the tumult of scandal, Nixon showed aggressive, attacking qualities in his relationships with others, using "Red-baiting"—accusing his political opponents of communist affiliation to discredit them. This served as a stepping stone to his own political success. In 1959, while vice president to Dwight Eisenhower, Nixon traveled to Moscow, where he jammed a warning finger into the chest of Russian Premier Nikita Krushchev during a debate. As vice-president, Nixon earned a measure of respect for his tough stance on the communists and other "un-Americans," reinforcing the congruence of his pointing mannerism with his personality.

A more contemporary pointer of note is Jesse Jackson. While virtually all the 1988 U.S. presidential candidates except Massachusetts Governor Michael Dukakis were obvious and flagrant pointers, Jackson appeared to be particularly outspoken with the silent signal. Neither the cautious "listen to me" point of George Bush nor the more emphatic "now get this" finger of Bob Dole were a match for the Jackson point. It isn't enough for Jackson to have a bullhorn to address a crowd, he has to point at it, too. Nicararguan leader Daniel

Fig. 5-6. Fidel Castro uses a pointing
finger like a whip.

Ortega seems to have learned a whipping or clubbing type of point from Fidel Castro (Figures 5-6 and 5-7), and Jesse jabs the sky with a similar weapon (Figure 5-8). Though according to *Time*, Rev. Jackson altered his approach from crusading, pulpit tactics to "hard-nosed" campaigning, he continued to look and act as if he were preaching.

Pointing is an angry signal that also warns or threatens. Gary Hart points a long digit skyward and seems to demand that his criticizing public recognize that "all of us are sinners." Perhaps he is trying to tell us that if we don't get off his case, our misdeeds will be discovered, too. Louis Farrakhan, leader of the Nation of Islam movement, wags a condescending finger of anti-Semitism from the lectern. Decent people should stay away from the dirtying influence of the Jews, he warns. Mo Kaddafi tilts his head back to add superiority connotations to his finger pointing after U.S. incursions into Libya. "Sting us, and

Fig. 5-7. Daniel Ortega pointing his finger. Are similar hand signals cultural?

Fig. 5-8. Jesse Jackson: Or is similarity in hand signals emotional?

Fig. 5-9. Reagan and Gorbachev: A handshake is a friendly gesture, but pointing is a warning. (Photo by Wally McNamee/ Newsweek)

we will bite you back a thousandfold," he seems to threaten. A vexed Tip O'Neill, former House Speaker, gestures with a furiously pointing finger and is censured for doing "hand-to-hand combat." Argentinian President Raul Alfonsin exhibits the clubbing or whipping style of point used by Castro and the other Central Americans to express his chagrin at an impasse with the International Monetary Fund. "Someone will have to 'give'," he growls. Then Soviet Foreign Minister Andrei Gromyko curls a pudgy hand into a fist and points while stating a hard Soviet line against the West. "...We will be able to stand up for ourselves..." against U.S. imperialism, was the ostensibly *counter-*belligerent message from the Kremlin in the early '80s.

Reagan and Gorbachev make interesting points. Gorbachev chats and smiles—and points. Reagan shakes hands and smiles—and points (Figure 5-9). Here the pointing finger seems to act like a toe testing the water. The set of gestures accompanying the point are clearly conciliatory, friendly: a smile, a handshake. The point itself says, "Don't think I'm a chump just because I'm being nice to you."

The Chopping Point

A variation on the pointing finger is a gesture reminiscent of a karate chop—the side of the hand used to emphasize a verbally communicate message. The significance of the chop is the same as the point: it signals frustration or emphasis, aggression or a threat. Since this gesture is a slightly softer form of emphasizer than the point or the fist, the chop may also signaify a promise rather than a threat. Walter Mondale, already noted as a fine nonverbal communicator, used the chop instead of the point or the fist (Figure 5-10).

Fig. 5-10. Walter Mondale's use of a chopping hand instead of a pointing finger adds emphasis but suggests greater self-control.

Summary: Frustration and Aggression Signals

Powerfulness and strong language or strong emotion are often confused. An emphatic person is frequently perceived as a strong person, but aggressiveness does not necessarily reflect strength of character, and the body language of a public figure can sometimes lend clues about this distinction. People who prominently display gestures involving pointing fingers and fisted hands may be signalling a belligerent and inappropriately aggressive personality. Such persons, while looking capable of wielding the reigns of power, are often in actuality not truly suited for leadership. The upraised fist of victory and success and the supporting, thoughtful fist of resolve are different from the whipping finger of a totalitarian or the angry, frustrated, sometimes pointing, often domineering fist of a dictator.

Gesture	Meaning
Upraised fist	Fearlessness, power, triumph, affirmation, possible despotism
Shaking the fist (the pounding fist)	Frustration, defensiveness, angry disagreement
Clasped fist	Highly negative sign, attempt to hold back frustration or anger. Lack of openness, untrustworthiness.
Holding the wrist of fisted hand	A power message, also holding back negative emotion

Gesture	Meaning
Fist to chin	Capacity for restraint, grim resolve, hardheadedness, possibly suppressed rage
A pointing finger	Frustration, a warning or a threat
Chopping gesture with side of hand	Same as the point but possibly milder

Notes on Nonverbal Communication: "Kicking the Dog"

Frustrated, aggressive individuals lack self-esteem and tend to use aggressive, attacking behaviors in a defensive way. Such people are threatened by anything less than total obedience. Blaming others, shaking a fist or a finger at them, pointing, and variations of "kicking the dog" are behaviors that may be indicative of an angry, frustrated personality with a poor sense of self.

CHAPTER 6

Decision Making and Integrity

If you can't convince them, confuse them
—Harry S. Truman

A critical function of politicians is to make decisions on behalf of their constituency. Decision making is a process that is clearly annotated by nonverbal language. By analysis of the gesture clues invariably and involuntarily emitted by people during the thought process, a trained and astute observer can often determine the outcome of an impending decision before the words telling about it are actually voiced.

The majority of signals that accompany the decision process involve touching one's own face. These can be broadly referred to as "hand to face" gestures. Hand to face gestures can be subdivided into those movements which signal thinking, evaluating, critiquing, deciding, doubting, and disbelieving.

Stroking the Chin

Stroking the chin, or touching the chin or cheek, is perhaps the most readily recognized of all decision-making gestures. Signifying thoughtfulness, the gesture indicates that a decision maker or evaluator is listening carefully, with great interest, while collecting or assessing data for an imminent decision. Rodin's famous statue in this pose seems wholly absorbed, lost in thought. Both 1984 Democratic

Fig. 6-1. John F. Kennedy: Holding or touching the chin reveals a thoughtful character.

vice-president hopefuls, Geraldine Ferraro and San Francisco Mayor Dianne Feinstein, were seen using the gesture. What could have been more thought-provoking in 1984 than a woman on the presidential ticket? Consumer advocate Ralph Nader, the careful representer of hidden facts, thoughtfully holds his chin, and late U.S. President John F. Kennedy, with his reputation for intelligence, was easily recognized by his thoughtful, hand to chin gesture (Figure 6-1).

When the hand of the gesturer is simply resting against cheek or chin, the decision-maker is taking in information with an open mind, listening. When the gesture changes to *stroking* the chin, the process changes from evaluation to decision-making. A negotiator or buyer who is observed to change from holding to stroking the chin is about to make a decision move. When the gesture changes from touching the chin or resting the chin lightly in the hand to supporting the weight of the head with the hand, the gesturer is loudly signalling boredom (Figure 6-2).

Fig. 6-2. Robert Bork: Holding the head up can be a sign of boredom.

Another gesture meaning thoughtfulness or concern is pinching the bridge of the nose (Figure 6-3). This movement is not seen as much in public as it is behind closed doors.

Critical Evaluation

A listener who holds or strokes the chin while someone else is making a presentation is generally favorably disposed toward what is being said. But extending a forefinger vertically alongside the cheek indicates the listener's mind has moved to a critical or even negative evaluation mode (Figure 6-4). A gesturer who supports the chin with a fist is not making a decision—the person's mind is already made up, and they will hold a hard line.

Peering over the tops of eyeglasses also has negative evaluation connotations, as discussed in Chapter 2. This gesture expresses a

Fig. 6-3. Pinching the bridge of the nose signals concern.

perspective of critical scrutiny in a largely negative light. When smokers are involved in decision-making, blowing smoke downward, toward the floor, makes a negative or critical statement about what is being said or the decision to be made.

Suspicion

Hand-to-face gestures are so much in evidence that nearly everyone wonders about them. Much of the contemporary research on body language was done by interviewing large numbers of people who were asked to observe videotaped interaction between people, during which specific gestures were enacted. A signal and its meaning became defined when a clear majority of viewers interpreted a given gesture in the same way.

Conversations between individuals are often accompanied by much rubbing, touching and pulling of the face. Especially suscep-

Fig. 6-4. Extending the forefinger vertically alongside the cheek suggests critical evaluation.

tible to the pull or rub are the eyes and nose. Nonverbal signals involving touches of the face have a two-way communication value. They can signal either a *received* emotion or perception, or a *transmitted* idea.

For example, touching or rubbing the nose generally signals suspicion. Rubbing by the speaker indicates suspicion or disbelief of the listener, or the speaker is not to be believed; a nose-rubbing listener distrusts what is being said, or distrusts the message sender. A lot of nose touching and ear-tugging can be seen during Senate debates. Perhaps this is a symbolic way of expressing, "I smell a rat."

Distrust, dislike, lying, doubt, and disbelief are all signalled, in context, by the hand-to-face gestures of rubbing or pulling at an eye or ear. Pulling at an eye may signal, "I just can't 'see' it that way," while pinching the ear is likely to mean something along the lines of, "I don't believe what I'm hearing." Haven't you ever tugged at one of your ears when you were about to say something that you thought the listener might not want to hear? Don't be surprised if you find yourself doing this privately next time you prepare to deliver an unpleasant message.

In the same way that disbelief, suspicion, or distrust are communicated by touching an eye or ear, lying involves touching gestures of the mouth. Covering the mouth while speaking is another body language tic that politicians are coached to avoid, but it slips out on occasion, nonetheless. A politician who covers the mouth while speaking may be expressing self-doubt—or telling a lie.

An angered general secretary of the Communist party, Mikhail Gorbachev, covered his mouth with one hand while balling the other into a fist after an angry outburst. A skeptical news anchorman, Tom Brokaw also covered his mouth while questioning Gorbachev in a famous interview. And Lt. Col. Oliver North steepled well-knit hands into a guard before his mouth during Iran-*contra* hearings (Figure 6-5). Did Ollie lie—or did someone else—or did North just not tell all that he knew? The particular "clasp and steeple" mouth-covering gesture of Oliver North suggests he kept his peace, not saying more than he did because he was confident that what he said was enough. Winston Churchill made a gesture similar to this to dodge a question at a press conference. Churchill smiled; North did not.

Agreement

Agreement and cooperation are valuable attitudes to secure when influencing the decisions of others. The face is not the only body part involved in nonverbal communication about decisions. When two people align their bodies in similar poses, they are said to be "mirroring," which indicates they are in agreement. At summit, when Reagan and Gorbachev faced each other with similar postures, they were likely to be in agreement, or close to agreement. Mirroring may involve legs that are crossed in the same way, or bodies that lean in the same direction. Mirroring often includes hands folded identically. When mirroring is present, either party could press for a commitment

Fig. 6-5. Oliver North: "Enough said!" (Photo by Wally Mc-Namee/Newsweek)

and would be more likely to reach accord than when mirroring is not in evidence.

President Reagan has acquired a powerful technique to keep shark reporters from getting too frenzied. During close interviews, he sits in a tight, proper posture with jacket neatly buttoned in front of his trim torso. His hands are folded quietly in his lap, from time to time pointing a finger as a warning that a question has come too close. Reagan's message: I am not open to criticism, boys (Figure 6-6).

Reagan's body language signals that he will not create openings for the reporters to attack, that he will not cooperate with attempts to make him uncomfortable. If he were to unbutton his jacket, the reporters would feel more at ease, sensing an attitude of willingness to cooperate on the part of the president. If Reagan would lean forward in his chair, reporters would sense he was interested in their views. If he would unfold his hands, refrain from pointing, and *show his palms as he spoke*, reporters might see him as open, honest, and sincere, and be less intent on catching him in a blunder (Figure 6-7).

Fig. 6-6. Ronald Reagan closed to criticism.

Palm Displays

The hallmark of peaceful intent and openness—in politics, in negotiations, in interpersonal relationships—is the display of the palm. An early form of salute, like the handshake, showing the palm indicates absence of malice, absence of a weapon. And when the palm is shown, people who see it are unconsciously relieved, made to feel at ease. A smart politician can have a tremendous impact on an audience by appropriate use of hand signals, especially those which reveal the palm.

To illustrate the power of the palm, imagine this scene: You are approaching an unfamiliar animal with whom you would like to make friends, such as your neighbor's dog. Very likely you would kneel to lower yourself to the pet's level and extend a wary hand for the pet to investigate. Having established a base of acceptance, you might reach out to pat the dog on the head. If you execute this maneuver by

Fig. 6-7. Reagan open to inquiry.

pushing your palm down over the dog's head, the animal is likely to wiggle away from you. If you modify your approach by turning your hand up, the dog may be more likely to let your hand approach. This is a primitive illustration of the power of the palm to put receivers of communication—human or animal—at ease.

If you've ever noticed that you seem to feel comfortable around certain people, but haven't been able to put your finger on a reason why, look for prominently displayed palms next time you encounter one of these "trust makers." As a psychologist, I have used this vital information at crucial points in therapy when I very much need the other person to lower their defenses and work with me cooperatively. If I am sitting back in my chair stroking my chin or with my hands comfortably steepled in my lap and I suddenly sit forward, rest my elbows on my thighs and separate my hands, dropping my fingers floorward with my palms facing toward the other person, I effectively add these messages to whatever else I say at the time: "I have been

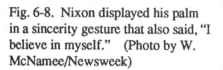
Fig. 6-8. Nixon displayed his palm in a sincerity gesture that also said, "I believe in myself." (Photo by W. McNamee/Newsweek)

listening very carefully to what you have been saying. I feel confident that I understand you. Now I'm going to tell you something very important. Please trust me." The combined effect of what I say verbally and how I augment it nonverbally are usually enough to generate the appropriate result.

Resigned U.S. president Richard Nixon flashed a lanky "high five" from the steps of his helicopter as he left Washington. By his action he silently but emphatically proclaimed, "I am not a crook," a phrase he was actually to voice soon after in a press conference. Nixon's uninhibited show of palm lent some credibility to his continued belief in himself (Figure 6-8).

Indeed, one of the reasons for Ronald Reagan's remarkable popularity in the United States today may well be his very liberal use of palm displays (Figure 6-9). How could anyone distrust a guy who is so genial, so disarming, so warm, and so comforting?

Fig. 6-9. Reagan's open palms are comforting; they lend an air of believability to what he has said.

Openly displayed, upwardly facing palms communicate sincerity and trustworthiness or believability. Democratic presidential hopeful Michael Dukakis, the governor from Massachusetts, may be stiff and stilted in his mannerisms, but he expresses himself in a way that supports the believability of what he says. When he addresses a crowd, his arms are spread wide, with palms open, up, and prominently displayed (Figure 6-10).

A palm display may also reflect blamelessness, even lack of responsibility. This is the sentiment behind the two-handed shrug: What, Me Worry? I don't even know the score (Figure 6-11).

Palms turned toward the floor send dominance signals, which will be explored a little more in a subsequent chapter. Palms turned up and in toward the gesturer, toward or even touching the chest or upper body of the speaker signify sincerity, honesty, trustworthiness, and submission. This is the body language of Oliver North in the presence

Fig. 6-10. Michael Dukakis's gesture
scores a point for integrity.

of William Casey, the deceased former CIA director. When Moshe
Arens, Israeli defense minister, visited the U.S. in 1984, he exhibited
open, palms up body language. Significant accommodations in U.S.-
Israeli relations were made during that trip. When first lady Nancy
Reagan met Raisa Gorbachev in Washington in 1987, it was obvious
from their body language that no love was lost between them. But
despite some catty remarks, Mrs. Reagan did use the palm-up-to-self
gesture to signal her sincere attempt to be gracious to her guest
(Figure 6-12).

In contrast to palm displays, someone who stands or walks with
one or both hands in a pocket may have a more retiring character than
someone who leaves the hands visible. The palm hider is likely to be
a person who "holds back" in any number of ways. A person who
negotiates with hand in pocket, for example, may have confidence,
but may also be holding something back, such as an undisclosed catch,
a trump, or an opinion. Henry Kissinger was noted for frequently
keeping a hand in a pocket (Figure 6-13).

Fig. 6-11. The classic shrug says,
"I'm not at fault."

Fig. 6-12. Nancy Reagan's body
language says, "Believe me. I mean
well." (Photo by W. McNamee/
Newsweek)

Fig. 6-13. Henry Kissinger's hand-in-pocket pose suggests that he's holding something back.

Summary: Decision-Making and Integrity

An important consideration for members of constituencies everywhere is the integrity and competence of the politicians entrusted with the task of decision-making and policy setting. A decision is the result of a process of subjecting information gathered over time to scrutiny and evaluation. A thoughtful, open-minded person is able to listen to the pros and cons of an argument, separate fact from opinion, and make a sound decision in the interests of the people they represent on the basis of personal integrity and flexible, intelligent analysis of the circumstances. Assessing the competence of a public figure may include critiquing their honesty, sincerity, and believability, as well as the process by which they arrive at conclusions.

Gesture	Meaning
Touching chin or cheek	Listening with interest, evaluating, taking in information, generally favorably
Stroking chin	Deciding, thoughtfulness
Pinching bridge of nose	Thoughtfulness or concern
Holding head up with hand	Boredom
Finger extended vertically alongside face	Critical or negative evaluation
Supporting chin with fist	A steadfast decision has been made
Peering over tops of glasses	Critical or judgmental evaluation
Blowing smoke downward —upward	Disagreement Agreement
Touching or rubbing the nose	Suspicion, not believing, or doubting what is heard
Pulling an eye or ear	Distrust, dislike, disbelief— either by listener or by speaker

Covering the mouth	Telling a lie or hearing a lie
Mirroring	Agreement, cooperation
Unbuttoned jacket	Openness, cooperation
Palm displays	Openness, peaceful intent, honesty, sincerity
Upward facing palms	Sincerity, trustworthiness, believability, blamelessness, lack of knowledge or responsibility (about wrongdoings)
Palms turned toward floor	Dominance
Palms to chest	Sincerity, honesty, trustworthiness, submission
Hands in pockets	Holding back, usually information, may be lying, but not necessarily

Notes on Nonverbal Communication:
Communication is a Two-Way Process

Communication implies a two-way process: transmitting and receiving. Often the gestures accompanying either side of a message are identical or similar. A person who is telling a lie, for example, may cover the mouth while speaking. The person who hears a falsehood may also cover the mouth as a gesture of disbelief, suspicion, or doubt. Evaluation gestures, which are *process* signals, must be assessed from both perspectives—as communication sender *or* receiver— before their congruence and meaning can be definitively declared.

CHAPTER 7

Press the Flesh

*Question: What does a gentleman do standing up, a lady
do sitting down and a dog do on three legs?*

Answer: Shake hands.

—The Turtle Society

The handshake has long been recognized as the signature of a person's character. It reveals much about people and about the interactions in which they are involved. A youth is reminded by his father to shake hands "like a man," while competitive handshakers use hand strength to signal powerfulness to a would-be adversary. And of course, politicians on the stump must "press the flesh" to contact their constituency. No other single body language signal not involving the face communicates as much as a handshake.

There are essentially five things to look for in interpreting a handshake: dominance, distance, strength of grip, barriers, and the use of more than one hand in the shake.

Dominance

The hand that is on top in any given handshake signifies the dominant party. The dominant handshaker is the one who is controlling the interaction, or is perceived by the other party to have more power. Dominance is established when one party extends a hand in a palm down position *and it is accepted this way by the other handshaker.*

Analysis of still photographs may not do justice to understanding a particular handshake because the dynamics of how the final clasp was reached are lost in the single, frozen frame. A hand extended palm down is not always or readily accepted that way, and handshakers engage in all sorts of gyrations to get their hand on top in a competitive power situation.

In October 1950, U.S. President Harry Truman met U.S. General Douglas MacArthur to congratulate the general on his Korean campaign. The two men locked together at the hand in what is likely to have been a powerful handshake. Though MacArthur's right hand was in the upper, dominant position at the moment of actual handshake, the president reached over the clasped hands and touched a medal on the general's chest with his left hand (Figure 7-1). While MacArthur's hand position relative to Truman's communicated an "I'm the boss" attitude or intention on the part of the military man, Truman's additional gesture allowed him to move in toward MacArthur, in a possible attempt to turn their hands over to regain dominance in

Fig. 7-1. Gen. Douglas MacArthur and President Harry Truman in a power struggle.

the interaction, a nonverbal "No you're not" retort. Less than a year after this October handshake, Truman fired MacArthur because the president felt the general was *too* aggressive.

There are exceptions to the dominant meaning of the upper hand. When a normally dominant person wishes to make a less powerful person feel at ease, a palm up hand may be extended. As covered in an earlier chapter, the display of the palm has a calming or comforting effect on people. Another exception occurs when a tall person shakes hands with a significantly shorter one. It would appear peculiar for the higher hand to approach the handshake palm up. Once contact has been made, an aggressive or dominant short person can turn the taller person's hand over, but with great disparities of height, it may be difficult to tell who really has the upper hand.

Distance

A whole subsection of body language is devoted to the study of interpersonal distances. "Proxemics" is a term coined by anthropologist Edward T. Hall to describe this study. Hall found that all people relate to others within zones of closeness or distance. Zones vary in size from zero (touching) to less than six inches, to twelve feet or more, depending on the nature of the interaction in which the people in the zone are engaged, the sex of the individuals involved, and the culture and upbringing of the individuals.

Women tend to stand closer together than men. An intimate male-female couple may stand closest of all. Asians and people in the Middle East stand closer than Americans. City dwellers are comfortable with less distance than are people who live in the country. Poor people of all nationalities stay close to each other when they congregate.

The handshake is fertile ground for judging interpersonal distance. Yes, all handshakers, by definition, must be close enough to touch, but how this touch is approached and sustained can be very revealing.

Aside from the cultural meaning, closeness in a handshake signifies either intimacy and warmth between the shakers, or aggression on the part of one or both. Friends and intimates stand close to each other; so do enemies. When Truman and MacArthur shook hands, in the example cited above, the two men were practically on top of each other. Given the sequel of the handshake, resulting in MacArthur's relief from duty, the physical closeness is likely to have signified a possible power struggle between the two leaders.

Distance between two shakers who are still connected at the hand signifies either distrust, aloofness, or reserve. Democratic presidential candidate Michael Dukakis, often criticized in the media for his lack of passion in his campaign style, tends to shake hands by planting his feet and extending his right arm out to meet the oncoming hand of the other shaker (Figure 7-2). This type of handshake is typical in rural areas. Dukakis is a suburbanite, but one who has earned a reputation as a cool headed businessman for his efforts as governor of Massachu-

Fig. 7-2. Dukakis reaching out and away from his body to shake hands maintains an emotional distance.

setts. His body language corroborates the cool, rational side of his character.

When Menachim Begin of Israel and Egyptian President Anwar Sadat shook hands at Camp David in 1978, a greater than natural distance was maintained during the shake. The significance of this distance is accentuated because citizens of middle eastern countries have a rather small public zone to begin with, resulting in considerable physical closeness during handshakes and conversations. The two mid-eastern leaders were brought together by U.S. President Jimmy Carter to discuss the possibility of peace between their respective countries, but there were many obstacles to overcome before an agreement could be reached between these two Biblical enemies. The first hurdle to overcome was that Begin's behavior while shaking hands clearly signalled that he simply did not trust Sadat.

Distance during a handshake can also be used manipulatively. In 1961, the young president of the United States, John F. Kennedy, met the infamous premier of the Soviet Socialist Republic, Nikita Krushchev. As do all good emissaries of peace, the two shook hands. Historically, shaking hands has signified peace by notifying the parties present that each comes without weapons. It is a statement of goodwill and, supposedly, trust. When Kennedy met Krushchev, both men eyed each other's offered hand with cautious scrutiny, rather than meeting each other eye to eye with an even gaze, as befits a statement of mutual trust and respect. Kennedy held his right arm back near his own body while opening his hand for the shake, functionally forcing the Soviet Premier to extend himself. Without uttering a word, the younger man stated, "You will have to come to me."

Just the opposite effect may be obtained by reaching aggressively into the personal space of another handshaker, especially with a palm down offer. This is tantamount to protesting too vigorously for acceptance or trust. Was this Krushchev's strategy? Probably not; Kennedy held the dominant hand position and it's not likely Krushchev purposely would have placed his hand in a submissive position relative to Kennedy's.

Strength of Grip

The strength of grip is an expression of individual character or situational intent. A powerful but compassionate person will offer a hand lightly and close on the hand of another only as firmly as the other does. This is to keep from hurting or frightening others with a display of superior strength. An aggressive or insecure person will purposely crunch another's hand.

Strategic Arms Reduction Talks (START) began with a U.S.-Soviet handshake in 1982. Five years later, the Americans and the Russians were still shaking hands over START. In December1987, Admiral William Crowe, chairman of the Joint Chiefs of Staff, met with Marshal Sergei Akhromeyev at the Pentagon. The two military men smiled broadly as they shook hands, but the smiles could have actually disguised pained grimaces: close observation of the ostensibly warm greeting revealed that Sergei was crushing Willie's fingers in what may have been a loudly contested, albeit wordless, power struggle (Figure 7-3).

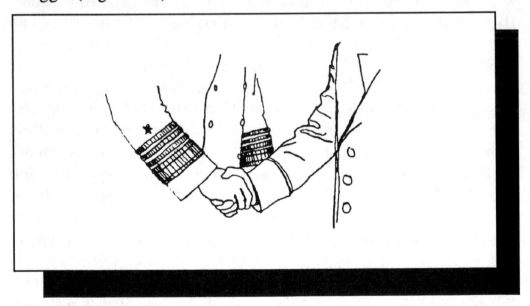

Fig. 7-3. An example of a "crushing" handshake.

Fig. 7-4. Woman usually dislike the fingertip squeeze form of handshake.

A weak grip suggests daintiness, civility, caution, or lack of personal vitality. In negotiations, a weak handshake is an acknowledgement of defeat. A person of integrity will shake firmly, evenly, looking into the eyes of the other, not squeezing the hand or holding it too lightly, but grasping it comfortably, without a sweaty palm.

Again, there is an exception to the dogma of "a firm grip means a firm personality." Many men have been taught, or have grown to believe, that shaking hands with a woman must be a tepid affair at best. In the interests of delicateness and mannerliness, they manfully grasp the fingertips of the lady's offered hand and gently, embracingly, squeeze. A man who does this can't be accused of lacking character on this basis alone. But most women *hate* getting their "tips squeezed" this way. It's often perceived as condescending, it feels awful, and the woman may tend to think the guy is a wimp (Figure 7-4). The proper way to shake hands with a woman is the same way as shaking hands with a man, without a "pump and crunch."

Barriers

In Chapter 2, the notion of barriers was introduced to describe objects or body parts that are placed between people involved in communication. The purpose of the barrier is to create a psychological defense or shield. Any object or body part placed inside the handshake, that is, between the two people shaking hands, bespeaks defensiveness and lack of trust.

Shoulders are placed inside a handshake by turning the body in silhouette or profile to the handshake. Akhromeyev did this while shaking hands with Crowe at START. A smile and a handshake are congruent communicators: they both signal goodwill. A handshake and a silhouette are incongruent, meaning they send differing messages; in this case, peaceful intent and distrust, respectively.

Eye contact is another important element of nondefensive handshaking. It is natural for handshakers to glance quickly at an extended hand to gauge distance when a handshake is initiated. Then, however, the gaze returns to and is held by the eyes. Otherwise trust is breached. A fascinating historical illustration of a hidden meaning or intent communicated by a handshake occurred at the 1945 Yalta meeting of "The Big Three": Roosevelt, Churchill, and Stalin. During the meeting, the capable diplomat, Averell Harriman, who was then the ambassador to Moscow, met and shook hands with Josef Stalin, a supposed ally. The shake was anything but friendly, it seemed, with Stalin blatantly silhouetting Harriman, both men powerfully locked at the hand, both men *actually looking away from each other* (Figure 7-5).

Papers are common objects placed inside a handshake. When Begin shook hands with Sadat at Camp David, he signalled his discomfort and distrust by maintaining a greater than normal distance while shaking, but also by keeping a sheaf of paper in his left hand prominently in front of his body.

In 1972, then U.S. President Richard Nixon met Soviet General Secretary Leonid Brezhnev. After signing a series of peaceful co-existence agreements, the two superpower leaders shook hands.

Fig. 7-5. Averell Harriman and Josef Stalin lack eye contact during this handshake meeting sending contradicting messages.

Whether by chance, accident, or intent, Nixon assumed the upper hand, palm-down position in the clasp, but the distinct impression in the eyes of watchful nonverbalists was that Nixon still did not trust Brezhnev. While Leonid kept his treaty booklets tucked under his left arm, Richard placed them squarely in the middle of the handshake (Figure 7-6) where they symbolically and simply communicated, "Yes we have agreed to friendly relations, but I still feel I need to protect myself from you." Whatever else he was, Nixon was an experienced statesman and a shrewd negotiator. His dominant hand position may have emphasized his conviction that he did not give away too much by agreeing to detente.

Two-handed Shake

The two-handed handshake is a controlling, manipulative gesture unless it is used between close friends, between doctor and patient, or

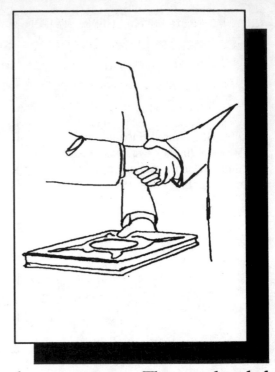

Fig. 7-6. A dominant handshake
with a protective barrier.

with a troubled person who needs reassurance. The two handed handshake is sometimes referred to as the politician's shake because it is a public figure's way of announcing instant intimacy. The two-handed handshake is intended to communicate sincerity. That doesn't make it always bad, as it may often be sincere. The Rev. Jesse Jackson, presidential hopeful, moves right in close to people, reaching out to touch them in the classic, two-handed politician's shake. In the pre-nomination polls Jackson was found to be a "believable" candidate.

But be alert to the silent message of manipulation the double handshake may contain. Unless used between communicators who are already familiar with each other, the double handshake often signals a desire to get oneself into the good graces of another, usually in a controlling fashion. Similarly, a right-handed shake accompanied by a left hand on the wrist, arm or shoulder of the other is a controlling gesture. The farther up the other person's arm the shaker's left hand, the more controlling is the significance of the gesture.

And finally, what could ooze more sincerity than a double double handshake? Both shakers committing to hand-on-hand-on-hand-on-hand is seen as regularly in political circles as a one-person double handshake. In December 1987, deposed monarch Prince Norodom Sihanouk of Cambodia met Hun Sen, prime minister of Cambodia, under the communist-controlled Heng Samrin regime. The meeting was intended to open doors of negotiation for a return to prominence of the prince as a bid for economic relief to the ravaged Cambodia. Certainly there is no love lost between Sihanouk and those currently in control of Cambodia. Nevertheless, when the prince and the prime minister met, they warmly clasped upon clasp, holding their four hands together like the very best of friends (Figure 7-7). Who needs most to ingratiate himself to whom in this complex scenario? Perhaps both need each other equally as desperately.

Likewise, when Argentine President Raul Alfonsin welcomed the irrepressible Isabel Peron, former president, back to the country as his guest, there was no crying Argentina in evidence. The two smilingly embraced hand-upon-hand (Figure 7-8). You could bet on the intentional sincerity of such a double double handshake. Alfonsin

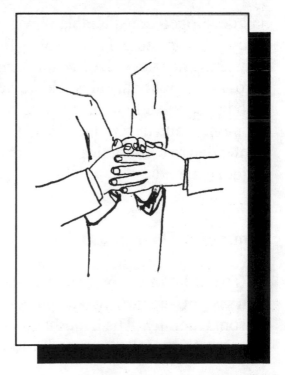

Fig. 7-7. A double-double handshake suggests sincerity and mutual benefit.

Fig. 7-8. Raul Alfonsin and Isabel Peron in a handshake that says, "I'll scratch your back if you'll scratch mine." Each politically needs the other. (Photo by Time Magazine)

had developed considerable power in Argentina via cunning diplomacy. By inviting Isabel home from her self-imposed exile and reinstating her as a citizen in good standing, he effectively courted the Peronists as political allies. He wanted the political clout that alliance with her was likely to bring. She wanted to come home to her land, her money, and her friends. While the covering or double handshake is intended to communicate warmth and sincerity, it often also covers a hidden agenda.

Summary: The Handshake

The point of studying the nonverbal behavior of politicians is to gain insight into the sum and process of their political know-how and personal identity. The handshake is a powerful nonverbal communicator which can tell many stories about a handshaker's self-image and capacity to project well in conflict situations. Symbolically, the handshake represents peace. In actuality, every handshake is a confrontation. And every confrontation, good or bad, has the potential to test a politician's mettle.

Gesture	Meaning
Hand on top in a handshake or extended palm down	Dominance, control
Turning the handshake over to get one's own hand on top	Striving for control, not accepting being controlled
Accepting a palm down handshake	Accepting the other person's authority
Offering a palm up handshake	Submission, conciliation. Also an attempt to make the other comfortable—a supporting gesture
Standing very close in a handshake	Either intimacy or enmity, possible cultural factors
Standing far apart in a handshake	Upbringing in a rural setting, emotional aloofness, coolness, lack of trust
Pulling the other party into one's own personal zone, or making them reach in	Controlling the other, controlling the interaction

Reaching in to another's personal zone	Aggressively controlling the other
Firm but comfortable grip	Integrity, self-confidence, sensitivity
Crushing the other's hand	Insecurity, aggression, power struggle, competition
Weak grip	A worn-out, or worn-down person, acknowledging defeat
Interposing a barrier into the handshake, e.g., papers or the right shoulder (silhouetting)	Defensiveness, distrust
Eye contact during handshake	Sincerity, openness, trust, self-confidence
Lack of eye contact	Insecurity, insincerity, distrust
Two handed handshake, one or both people	"Instant intimacy" between strangers, sincerity, attempt to comfort and support, possible manipulation and/or attempt to control
Left hand on wrist, elbow or shoulder while shaking hands	Attempt to control the other

CHAPTER 8

Checklist of Executive Qualities

As I grow older, I pay less attention to what
men say. I just watch what they do.

—*Andrew Carnegie*

Of all the gestures, postures, and mannerisms explored in this book, which are critical indicators to look for when observing a public figure? So many of the movements people display while speaking are irrelevant to their actual message. How do you sort it all out?

This chapter contains a checklist of approximately thirty prominent gestures in 14 broad categories that will help you organize your observation and assessment of the communication integrity of political figures. Each category has a heading, with its related gestures listed underneath. The entire checklist is divided along the dimension of "desirable" or "undesirable" according to the impact of a given trait on performance in the public sector. You can keep the checklist nearby as you listen and watch a speech or public appearance. Perhaps this information will afford you some insight into the personality, integrity, believability, and competence of the would-be history-maker before you.

The checklist is not exhaustive; it is intended only to highlight prominent mannerisms, and only those mannerisms that have more or less direct bearing on essential leadership qualities.

CHECKLIST OF EXECUTIVE QUALITIES

DESIRABLE	UNDESIRABLE
Confidence	**Defensiveness**
__ The Figure Four	__ Crossed arms in front of chest
__ Hands on hips	
__ Thumbs hooked in belt	__ Crossed arms with "clutching"
__ "Thumbs up" gestures	__ Tightly crossed legs or locked ankles or knees
__ Steepling	
__ Subtle steepling	__ Straddling backwards chair
__ Firm but comfortable handshake with good eye contact	__ Peering over eyeglasses
	__ Use of silhouettes or barriers in handshakes

DESIRABLE	UNDESIRABLE
Authority	**Worry, Self-Doubt, Need for Reassurance**
__ Hands clasped behind back	__ Clasping
	__ Holding one's own hand or wrist
Resolve, Conviction Self-Control	**Excess Aggression, Frustration**
__ Fist to chin	__ Angry fist gestures (fist as hammer or club, shaking the fist); holding a fist
	__ Pointing a finger
	__ Excess grip strength in hand-shake
Listening, Considering	**Deceit**
__Touching or stroking the chin	__ Covering mouth while talking

DESIRABLE	**UNDESIRABLE**
Agreement, Cooperation __ Mirroring	
Sincerity, Openness __ Palm displays	
Dominance __ Upper hand in handshake	**Insecurity** __ Use of silhouettes and barriers, especially in handshakes
Congruence __ Sameness in verbal and nonverbal message suggests integrity	**Incongruence** __ Difference in verbal and nonverbal message suggests dishonesty

CHAPTER 9

The End of the Race

*No matter how humble a man's beginnings, he
achieves the status of the office to which he
is elected.*
                              —Nikita Krushchev

Politicians are as much maligned as the Internal Revenue Service
and the Postal Service in the United States, yet each has tremendous
value in the workings of society. Still, if one could get even with the
IRS....

How to avenge yourself on the tax collectors is not the concern of
this book, but evening up the disadvantages that voters encounter
when faced with image-managed public figures is. Now you have a
broad library of information with which to appraise every public
address of every politician you observe. You have body language
clues to a person's intent and character even when their words may be
cleverly disguising true meanings. The "Notes on Nonverbal Communication" at the end of most of the chapters contain insights about
the motivation behind public behavior, and insight into the significance of these motivations. Before you cast a ballot you can evaluate
your favorite and be confident that you are basing your choice on the
real competencies of the person, not just what that person wants you
to believe.

Not every gesture will fit the meanings developed in this book
every time you see it displayed. Remember the "Three C's of
Nonverbal Communication": context, clusters, and congruence.
Always take into consideration *where* a communication is taking

place, and what its significance or intent is supposed to be. Be sure to look for *groups* of gestures that logically and consistently hang together, rather than basing your assessment on any single signal—a surefire way to be misled.

Finally, check the congruence of every communication you assess: does the gesture fit the message? Is what you're perceiving consistent with the other things you know about this particular speaker? Is the speaker orating magnificently about peace and brotherly love while lying with body gestures? When Oscar Arias presented his Nobel Peace Prize winning proposition to the United States, his body language screamed anything *but* believability, credibility, diplomacy, or honesty. Yet we feel certain that this man sincerely longs for peaceful accord in Central America. In a case like this, it may be worthwhile to withhold strict judgment based on analysis of body language, opting instead to: a) judge the man on his merits; b) let the facts speak for themselves; or c) wait and see what happens.

Yes, some politicians may be skillful and cagey enough to fool even educated nonverbalists. Especially because communication in the political realm is so complex, it is difficult and risky to attach definitive meanings to specific or isolated events without allowing for exceptions, more so than in other settings. For the most part, if you apply your new knowledge of body language intelligently and systematically, you will be able to tell if the person you are observing is being truthful; look for the appearance of openness signals such as palm displays. If the person is attempting to deceive, you are likely to see prominent anxious, defensive, or "closed" signals like crossed arms or legs, a covered mouth, clasped or clenched hands, or a "tight" posture. You have learned to look for the dominance and confidence signals that indicate leadership: positive thumb gestures and upper-handedness in handshakes, for example.

You are able to quickly spot "red flags" of personality, such as despotism and unbridled aggression, that foretell tumult and chaos.

Thus, you have a tool now to help you develop your political opinion via an informed analysis of the major characters involved in a given scenario. You may even be able to judge the intelligence and integrity of a political figure, simply by observing their body language, by looking for the process gestures of thoughtfulness, and by watching the quality of an individual's interactions with others.

There are some caveats of which to beware as you begin to use the information in this book. Keep in mind that the expressions, gestures, postures, mannerisms, and movements developed in the preceding pages are expressly devoted to nonverbal communication in the political arena. A woman who brings her open palm to her chest, as did Nancy Reagan when meeting with Raisa Gorbachev at the White House, may be signalling something very different from sincerity and graciousness when the signal is emitted in a threat situation. Typically, this is a symbolic, self-defense gesture most often used by women, but in the world of politics, the action can be used to illustrate a range of intent, from the most hospitable welcome to a deceptive fake: "Lie to you? No, not *me,* not *ever,*" is a common manipulative, political use of this otherwise innocuous, even positive signal. Likewise, an upraised fist by the winner of an arduous athletic competition signifies something quite apart from the almost sinister gloating expressed by the upraised fist of a Manuel Noriega failing to be unseated by political pressure.

Politics, by definition, is comprised of peculiarly circumscribed, formalized behaviors and relationships. Rules of conduct, *accepted* conduct, are different in governance than they are in other arenas. In politics there is greater leeway for artful manipulation and cunning. The shrewd politician may be the most successful in terms of influence and longevity with a constituency, even though such a person may not be the best one for the job. In the same vein, the politician with the best image management may be the most successful, and in politics, more so than in any other field except entertainment, *nonverbal behavior is carefully coached and developed to create an effect.*

Body language the casual observer witnesses among politically active public figures is likely to differ in meaning from what identical gestures signify in other contexts.

Take the simple, prominent, highly visible gesture of arms crossed in front of the body as an example. In Chapter 2 on Defensiveness, we discussed the trend in modern politics to resist the urge to display this gesture, as psychologically it tends to convey a message of insecurity, rigidity, and closed mindedness, all of which are considered undesirable in terms of gaining popular support. On the other hand, the very same gesture has been used in politics to express fortitude, conviction, and statesmanlike power, so it is often selected as the pose of choice for political portraits.

Politics, the business of government, is a game with a long, illuminated history. Like any other game, there is a specific objective in politics: winning. As in any other game, there are rules, strategies, tactics, and practice that contribute to the successful attainment of the objective. Oratory and influence are central implements of the political game. To communicate effectively means an increased likelihood of winning, and every successful politician knows what you know now, too: that body language speaks as loudly, as passionately, as persuasively as any verbal communication. Politicians know this and are trained to use this knowledge to accomplish their aims. Now that you know it, you can use it, too, to help you cut to the heart of the matter and hear the truth—the silent speech of politicians.

Fig. 3-7. Michael Dukakis uses his thumbs to reassure the public that he is confident.

Fig. 3-8. President Reagan uses his thumb to signal victory.

Fig. 3-9. Jesse Jackson's thumbs-up signal says, "I feel good. Why not join me?"

Fig. 3-10. "Thumbing," or "jerking the thumb:" an adult put-down.

Fig. 3-11. Churchill's famous "V for Victory" gesture also signals self-confidence.

Fig. 3-12. Nixon adopted Churchill's confidence gesture and made it his own trademark.

Fig. 3-13. The high steeple demonstrates strong expressive confidence.

Fig. 3-14. The steepled fingers of Mikhail Gorbachev signals quiet self-confidence.

Fig. 3-15. While listening, Gorbachev's lower steeple suggests a receptive, but confident frame of mind.

Fig. 3-16. Lt. Col. Oliver North's folded steeple speaks silently of self-confidence.

Fig. 3-17. Churchill in an elegant modified steeple radiates self-confidence.

Fig. 4-1. The tightly clasped hands of Frank Carlucci suggest inner tension or worry.

Fig. 4-2. Nixon's "Hand-in-Front-of-Body" clasp could have been an anxiety signal.

Fig. 4-3. Kurt Waldheim in his own version of the "Hand-in-Front-of-Body" clasp.

Fig. 4-4. Holding a fist with the other hand suggests frustration or aggression.

Fig. 4-5. Michael Jackson's clasped hands say silently that, despite his ability to perform on stage, he is really an introvert.

Fig. 4-6. Hidden fingers suggest a hidden agenda.

Fig. 4-7. Holding her own hand, Geraldine Ferraro seems to be seeking reassurance.

Fig. 4-8. When clasping shifted to steepling, you knew Ferraro had become confident.

Fig. 4-9. The "Hands-Behind-the-Back" pose of George Schultz is typical of people who believe in their own authority.

Fig. 4-10. The "Hands-Behind-Head" pose of Arnold Schwarzennegger signifies a very high degree of self confidence, possibly to the point of arrogance.

Fig. 4-11. The clasp and steeple is an aggressive superiority gesture.

Fig. 5-1. In 1968, American Olympic medalists gave the salute of power gesture.

Fig. 5-2. Adolf Hitler's agitated fist added emphasis to his agitated words.

Fig. 5-3. Manuel Noreiga's upraised fist suggests an angry tyrant.

Fig. 5-4. The way Kadaffi holds his fist by the other hand is a negative sign. It means anger is present and is barely held back.

Fig. 5-5. Holding the fist may suggest a person has something to hide, or is trying to hide angry feelings.

Fig. 5-6. Fidel Castro uses a pointing finger like a whip.

Fig. 5-7. Daniel Ortega pointing his finger. Are similar hand signals cultural?

Fig. 5-8. Jesse Jackson: Or is similarity in hand signals emotional?

Fig. 5-9. Reagan and Gorbachev: A handshake is a friendly gesture, but pointing is a warning.

Fig. 5-10. Walter Mondale's use of a chopping hand instead of a pointing finger adds emphasis but suggests greater self-control.

Fig. 6-1. John F. Kennedy: Holding or touching the chin reveals a thoughtful character.

Fig. 6-2. Robert Bork: Holding the head up can be a sign of boredom.

Fig. 6-3. Pinching the bridge of the nose signals concern.

Fig. 6-4. Extending the forefinger vertically alongside the cheek suggests critical evaluation.

Fig. 6-5. Oliver North: "Enough said!"

Fig. 6-6. Ronald Reagan closed to criticism.

Fig. 6-7. Reagan open to inquiry.

Fig. 6-8. Nixon displayed his palm in a sincerity gesture that also said, "I believe in myself."

Fig. 6-9. Reagan's open palms are comforting; they lend an air of believability to what he has said.

Fig. 6-10. Michael Dukakis's gesture scores a point for integrity.

Fig. 6-11. The classic shrug says, "I'm not at fault."

Fig. 6-12. Nancy Reagan's body language says, "Belive me. I mean well."

Fig. 6-13. Henry Kissinger's hand-in-pocket pose suggests that he's holding something back.

Fig. 7-1. Gen. Douglas MacArthur and President Harry Truman in a power struggle.

Fig. 7-2. Dukakis reaching out and away from his body to shake hand maintains an emotional distance.

Fig. 7-3. An example of a "crushing" handshake.

Fig. 7-4. Women usually dislike the fingertip squeeze form of handshake.

Fig. 7-5. Averell Harriman and Josef Stalin lack eye contact during this handshake meeting, sending contradicting messages.

Fig. 7-6. A dominant handshake with a protective barrier.

Fig. 7-7. A double-double handshake suggests sincerity and mutual benefit.

Fig. 7-8. Raul Alfonsin and Isabel Peron in a handshake that says, "I'll scratch your back if you'll scratch mine." Each politically needs the other.

BIBLIOGRAPHY

Birdwhistell, Ray L. <u>Introduction to Kinesics.</u> Louisville, Ky: The University of Louisville Press, 1952.

Bowmen, John. <u>Pictorial History of the American Presidency</u>. N.Y: W. H. Smith, 1986.

Churchill, Rudolph S. & Gernsheim, Helmut (eds.) <u>Churchill: His Life in Photographs</u>. N.Y: Rinehart & Co., 1955

Darwin, Charles. <u>The Expression of Emotion in Man and Animals</u>. Chicago: The University of Chicago Press, 1965.

Fast, Julius. <u>Body Language</u>. Philadelphia: Evans & Co.,1970.

Hall, E. T. <u>Silent Language</u>. N.Y: Doubleday, 1959.

Mar, Timothy T. <u>Face Reading: The Chinese Art of Physiognomy</u>. N.Y: Dodd, Mead & Co., 1974

Nierenberg, G. I. <u>The Art of Negotiating</u>. N.Y: Hawthorn Books, 1968.

Nierenberg, G. I. & Calero, H. <u>How to Read a Person Like a Book</u>. N.Y: Pocket Books, 1971.

Pease, Allan. <u>Signals: How to Use Body Language for Power, Success and Love</u>. N.Y: Bantam, 1984.

Scheflen, A. E. "Significance of Posture in Communications Systems." Psychiatry, 27, 4, 1964.

Speer, Albert. Inside the Third Reich. Translated by Richard and Clara Winston. N.Y: Macmillan, 1970.

INDEX